NVIDIA

The Story of Three Visionaries Who Built a Visual
Computing Empire

JEREMY MITCHELL

TABLE OF CONTENTS

Introduction

In the vast and rapidly evolving world of technology, few companies have had the kind of transformative impact that Nvidia has. From its humble beginnings as a startup with a bold vision, Nvidia has grown into a global powerhouse that has redefined industries and reshaped the future of computing. Whether you're a gamer who has marveled at the stunning realism brought to life by Nvidia's graphics cards, a scientist leveraging the computational power of GPUs to unravel the mysteries of the universe, or a business leader embracing the potential of artificial intelligence, chances are that Nvidia has touched your life in ways you might not even realize.

This book delves into the remarkable story of Nvidia, a company that began with a simple idea: to create a chip that could bring 3D graphics to life. From that initial concept, Nvidia has not only dominated the graphics processing industry but has also ventured into uncharted territories, becoming a key player in fields as diverse as artificial intelligence, autonomous vehicles, healthcare, and data science.

Nvidia's journey is one of relentless innovation, strategic foresight, and a deep understanding of the future needs of technology. It is a story of how a small team of visionaries, led by the charismatic and determined Jensen Huang, navigated the complex and competitive tech landscape to build a company that would become synonymous with cutting-edge graphics and AI. Along the way, Nvidia faced numerous challenges—from fierce competition and legal battles to the ever-present pressure to stay ahead in an industry defined by constant change. Yet, time and again, Nvidia has proven its ability to adapt, innovate, and thrive.

As you explore the chapters ahead, you will discover how Nvidia's pioneering work in GPUs laid the foundation for its expansion into new areas, ultimately positioning it at the forefront of the AI revolution. You will learn about the strategic decisions that fueled Nvidia's growth, the innovations that set it apart from its competitors, and the impact it has had on industries across the globe.

But this book is not just a chronicle of Nvidia's rise to prominence; it is also a glimpse into the future. Nvidia's influence is far from over, and the company's vision for the future—whether in the realms of AI, the metaverse, or beyond—promises to continue shaping the world in ways we can only begin to imagine.

In telling the story of Nvidia, this book offers insights not only into the company itself but also into the broader technological shifts that have defined the modern era. It is a story of ambition, innovation, and the relentless pursuit of excellence—a story that serves as both a testament to what Nvidia has achieved and a preview of what lies ahead.

Chapter 1:
Founding Nvidia

The Visionaries Behind Nvidia

The story of Nvidia begins with three visionaries whose backgrounds, talents, and aspirations would converge to create a company that would revolutionize computing and graphics. Jensen Huang, Chris Malachowsky, and Curtis Priem were not just engineers; they were pioneers driven by a shared belief in the transformative potential of technology. Their combined expertise laid the foundation for Nvidia's ascent to become a global leader in graphics processing and AI.

Jensen Huang: The Visionary Leader

Jensen Huang, the visionary co-founder and driving force behind Nvidia, was born in Taiwan in 1963. His early life in Taiwan provided him with a foundation rooted in traditional values and academic excellence. At the age of nine, Huang and his family emigrated to the United States, where they settled in Oneida, Kentucky—a small, rural town that stood in stark contrast to the bustling urban environment of Taipei. For a young Huang, this move marked the beginning of a new chapter in his life, one defined by a series of challenges that would shape his future as a technologist and entrepreneur.

One of the earliest challenges Huang faced was adapting to a completely different culture and language. The rural surroundings of Oneida presented an entirely new way of life, and like many immigrant children, Huang had to quickly learn English while navigating the social and academic dynamics of American schools. Despite these obstacles, his resilience and natural intellectual curiosity helped him excel. He quickly distinguished himself as an exceptional student with a profound aptitude for mathematics and science—subjects in which he displayed an innate talent.

Huang's academic excellence continued throughout high school, where he developed a growing interest in how technology could reshape the world. This fascination with technology led him to pursue a degree in electrical engineering at Oregon State University. It was here that Huang began to cultivate his passion for computer architecture, one of the fields that would eventually underpin his groundbreaking work at Nvidia. His undergraduate years were marked by hard work, a drive for innovation, and a hunger to understand the complexities of computing at a deeper level.

After earning his bachelor's degree in electrical engineering, Huang set his sights on furthering his education at Stanford University, one of the world's leading institutions for engineering and technology. At Stanford, Huang earned a master's degree in electrical engineering, and it was during this period that he deepened his understanding of the rapidly evolving technology landscape. Stanford's dynamic academic environment provided Huang with exposure to cutting-edge research and the opportunity to collaborate with some of the brightest minds in the field. This experience further refined his technical expertise and broadened his perspective on the potential of computing.

Huang's early career was equally formative, as he gained invaluable experience working at some of the most prominent companies in the semiconductor and technology industries. His first major role was at Advanced Micro Devices (AMD), where he worked on microprocessor design. This role gave him hands-on experience with the complexities of chip design and exposed him to the intense competition within the semiconductor industry. Huang's work at AMD allowed him to understand the intricate balance between innovation and market demand in a field where advancements in microprocessor design could make or break a company's success.

Following his time at AMD, Huang moved to LSI Logic, a company known for its expertise in custom silicon design. At LSI, he worked on system-on-chip (SoC) solutions, a technology that would later become a cornerstone of Nvidia's product lineup. SoC technology integrates all components of a computer or electronic system into a single chip, improving efficiency and performance. This experience proved instrumental in shaping Huang's future vision for Nvidia, as it gave him a deeper understanding of how hardware could be optimized for specific applications.

While his technical skills were formidable, Huang's entrepreneurial spirit truly set him apart. In the early 1990s, he became deeply interested in 3D graphics—a nascent field at the time, with enormous untapped potential. The concept of 3D graphics was still in its infancy, but Huang saw a future where computing would be increasingly visual, with applications that extended far beyond gaming. He believed that graphics processing would become a central component of computing devices, enabling richer, more immersive user experiences in everything from entertainment to scientific visualization.

Huang's vision was bold: to create a chip that could handle complex graphics computations in real-time, dramatically enhancing the visual capabilities of computers. His conviction was that the future of computing would be shaped by visual interaction, and that the industry needed specialized hardware capable of meeting these new demands. This vision would later become the cornerstone of Nvidia's mission and guide the company's growth from a small startup to a global leader in GPU (Graphics Processing Unit) technology.

In 1993, Jensen Huang, along with Chris Malachowsky and Curtis Priem, co-founded Nvidia with the goal of building that specialized chip. The trio shared a belief that 3D graphics would revolutionize computing, and their complementary skills made them a formidable team. Huang, with his background in chip design and strong leadership, took on the role of CEO—a position he has held since the company's inception.

The early days of Nvidia were challenging. The company faced stiff competition from well-established players in the semiconductor industry, and raising capital was no easy feat. However, Huang's unwavering belief in Nvidia's vision kept the company focused, even when the road ahead seemed uncertain. He personally drove Nvidia's efforts to secure funding, build a talented team, and refine its technology. Under Huang's leadership, Nvidia released its first major product, the NV1, in 1995—a 3D graphics chip that, although not a commercial success, laid the foundation for the company's future innovations.

It was this persistence, guided by Huang's visionary leadership, that eventually led to Nvidia's breakthrough with the GeForce 256 in 1999—the world's first GPU. The GeForce 256 revolutionized the gaming industry and established Nvidia as a major player in the tech world. The success of the GPU was not just a technical victory, but a validation of Huang's belief that visual computing would be central to the future of technology.

Beyond his technical expertise, Huang's leadership style has been a critical factor in Nvidia's sustained success. Known for his hands-on approach and commitment to innovation, Huang fosters a corporate culture that prioritizes research and development. He encourages experimentation, giving engineers the freedom to explore bold ideas while maintaining a focus on delivering products that push the boundaries of what is possible. Under Huang's guidance, Nvidia has continued to innovate, developing technologies like real-time ray tracing, AI-driven graphics enhancements, and data center solutions that have had far-reaching implications across industries.

Huang's entrepreneurial drive and ability to adapt to shifting technological trends have allowed Nvidia to expand beyond its core graphics market. Today, Nvidia is a leader not only in gaming and graphics but also in AI, deep learning, and autonomous systems. The company's GPUs are used in supercomputers, medical research, automotive AI, and data centers, making Nvidia a critical player in the broader tech ecosystem.

Jensen Huang's story is one of vision, perseverance, and relentless pursuit of innovation. From his humble beginnings in Taiwan to leading one of the world's most influential technology companies, Huang's journey reflects a deep commitment to pushing the boundaries of what is possible in computing. His belief that the future of technology would be visual, and his ability to turn that belief into reality through Nvidia, has had a transformative impact on industries and society as a whole. Today, Nvidia continues to shape the future of computing, driven by Huang's leadership and his unwavering focus on innovation.

Chris Malachowsky: The Engineering Powerhouse
Chris Malachowsky, one of the three co-founders of Nvidia, played an integral role in shaping the company's vision and technological breakthroughs. Born in 1959, Malachowsky had a natural curiosity for technology and engineering from a young age. This passion led him to pursue a degree in electrical engineering at the University of Florida, where he gained a solid foundation in electronics, computing, and system design. His education equipped him with the theoretical knowledge and problem-solving skills essential for

navigating the rapidly evolving tech landscape of the late 20th century.

After graduating, Malachowsky embarked on his career at Hewlett-Packard (HP), a company with a legacy of innovation in computing and electronics. At HP, he worked on high-performance computing (HPC) systems, an area that focuses on creating machines capable of processing vast amounts of data in real-time for scientific and industrial purposes. His role at HP provided him with hands-on experience in designing and optimizing complex computer architectures. It was here that he became intimately familiar with the challenges of building systems that could handle large-scale, intricate computations quickly and efficiently—a skill set that would prove pivotal in his future work at Nvidia.

Malachowsky's work at HP centered around systems for scientific computing, a field that requires precision and computational power far beyond that of standard computing systems. He was responsible for developing architectures that could meet the demands of complex simulations and data processing tasks in fields like physics, climate modeling, and other scientific research areas. The experience he gained at HP gave him a deep understanding of both hardware and software design, as well as the performance limitations of existing computing solutions at the time.

During his time at HP, Malachowsky also developed a strong interest in parallel computing, a paradigm that seeks to increase computational speed and efficiency by dividing tasks across multiple processors to work on simultaneously. This concept, which was relatively new in the 1980s and early 1990s, intrigued Malachowsky because of its potential to vastly improve performance in data-heavy applications, particularly graphics. His fascination with parallel computing would become a driving force in his later contributions to Nvidia's pioneering GPU technology, where parallel processing would play a central role in enabling the rapid rendering of 3D graphics.

Malachowsky's technical expertise was complemented by his ability to foster teamwork and collaboration among engineers. He believed that some of the best technological innovations could emerge from collective problem-solving, where diverse perspectives could converge to tackle complex issues. This mindset became a key element of Nvidia's corporate culture and was crucial in the company's early days, as it worked on developing revolutionary technology with limited resources.

When Malachowsky co-founded Nvidia in 1993 with Jensen Huang and Curtis Priem, his engineering background and industry experience became invaluable assets. His work on high-performance systems at HP had exposed him to the kinds of computational challenges Nvidia sought to address in the realm of 3D graphics. Nvidia's goal was to create a new class of chips specifically designed to handle graphics processing more efficiently than traditional CPUs could—a task that required the integration of hardware and software knowledge, something Malachowsky was uniquely equipped to do.

In the early years of Nvidia, Malachowsky focused heavily on the technical side of the business, contributing to the design of Nvidia's early graphics processing units (GPUs) and helping build the engineering team that would turn the company's vision into reality. His insights into parallel computing were particularly critical in the development of the company's first products, as GPUs fundamentally rely on parallel processing to render graphics in real-time. His collaborative approach also helped foster a culture of innovation within Nvidia, where engineers were encouraged to push the boundaries of what was possible with the available technology.

One of the most significant contributions Malachowsky made to Nvidia was his work on the GeForce series of GPUs, which would become the company's flagship product line. The GeForce 256, released in 1999, is widely recognized as the world's first GPU—a groundbreaking innovation that set Nvidia apart from its competitors and established the company as a leader in graphics technology. Malachowsky's understanding of the need for efficient parallel processing was instrumental in the development of this product, which revolutionized the gaming industry and expanded the possibilities of computer graphics.

Beyond gaming, the work Malachowsky contributed to Nvidia also laid the groundwork for the company's expansion into other industries that rely on high-performance computing. The GPUs that Malachowsky helped design would eventually be used in data centers, scientific research, AI, and even autonomous vehicles, demonstrating the far-reaching impact of his technical expertise and vision. His early contributions to Nvidia's engineering culture and technological foundation continue to influence the company's trajectory to this day.

Malachowsky's career at Nvidia exemplifies the fusion of technical expertise, forward-thinking vision, and collaborative leadership. His background in high-performance computing and parallel processing, combined with his hands-on experience at HP, allowed him to foresee the transformative potential of GPUs long before they became a cornerstone of modern computing. His role in co-founding Nvidia, alongside Jensen Huang and Curtis Priem, was pivotal in the company's early success and its rise to prominence as a leader in the tech industry.

Today, Chris Malachowsky continues to serve as a senior technology leader and mentor within Nvidia, helping guide the company as it pushes the boundaries of innovation in artificial intelligence, gaming, autonomous driving, and more. His legacy as an engineer and entrepreneur is evident in Nvidia's continued dominance in the graphics and computing space, where the principles of parallel processing and high-performance computing that he championed remain central to the company's strategy..

Curtis Priem: The Architect of Graphics

Curtis Priem, the third co-founder of Nvidia, played a crucial role in the company's foundational innovations in graphics processing. Born in 1957, Priem was deeply interested in technology and design from a young age, eventually pursuing a degree in electrical engineering at Rensselaer Polytechnic Institute (RPI). His education at RPI provided him with a strong foundation in computer systems, digital design, and hardware architecture, preparing him for a career in the cutting-edge world of computer graphics.

After completing his degree, Priem began his professional journey at IBM, one of the world's leading technology companies. At IBM, Priem contributed to a number of projects that would shape the future of personal computing, most notably the development of the first graphics processor for PCs. His work involved designing systems that could handle the increasing graphical demands of personal computers, which were quickly becoming central to both business and entertainment industries. This role gave Priem invaluable insights into the challenges and complexities of graphics processing, as well as the opportunities that new technologies could unlock.

Priem's experience at IBM was groundbreaking, especially at a time when computer graphics were still in their infancy. His contributions to early graphics processors laid the foundation for what would later become a core technology in Nvidia's products. The experience also gave him a deep understanding of how graphics hardware could be optimized for performance, something that would prove instrumental in Nvidia's future success.

Following his tenure at IBM, Priem moved to Sun Microsystems, another major player in the computing world known for its innovations in workstations and network computing. At Sun, Priem continued to work in the field of graphics, focusing on high-performance graphics systems for workstations. Sun Microsystems was renowned for its powerful hardware, and Priem's role allowed him to refine his expertise in creating graphics systems capable of handling the demanding needs of professional users in industries like engineering, design, and animation.

Priem's work at Sun further solidified his reputation as an expert in graphics processing, and he gained extensive experience designing systems that could handle large-scale graphical computations. His time at Sun was also an important stepping stone in his career, as it prepared him for the leap into entrepreneurship that would come with the founding of Nvidia.

When Priem co-founded Nvidia in 1993 alongside Jensen Huang and Chris Malachowsky, he brought with him a wealth of knowledge in graphics architecture. His background in designing cutting-edge graphics systems for both IBM and Sun gave him a unique perspective on how to tackle the technical challenges Nvidia would face as it set out to create a new class of graphics processing units (GPUs). Priem's expertise was particularly crucial in Nvidia's early years, as the company was striving to create a chip that could handle the complex graphical demands of the emerging 3D computing era.

Priem's vision for Nvidia aligned perfectly with the company's mission. He believed, like Huang, that the future of computing would be driven by visual experiences. In an era when most computing power was dedicated to processing text and numbers, Priem saw an opportunity to revolutionize the way computers handled visual data. His deep understanding of graphics architecture and parallel processing allowed him to play a key role in designing Nvidia's early GPUs, which were built to handle the increasingly complex graphical needs of applications like video games, professional design software, and scientific simulations.

Priem's passion for pushing the boundaries of what was possible with graphics technology was instrumental in shaping Nvidia's early product offerings. His work on the company's first GPUs set the stage for Nvidia's eventual dominance in the field of graphics processing. Under his guidance, Nvidia developed products that were not only powerful but also highly efficient, capable of handling the intricate demands of real-time 3D rendering.

One of Priem's most significant contributions to Nvidia was his involvement in the development of the GeForce 256, released in 1999. The GeForce 256 is widely recognized as the world's first GPU, a revolutionary piece of technology that changed the landscape of computer graphics forever. Priem's expertise in graphics architecture was critical in the design and implementation of the GeForce 256, which introduced a new era of performance and capability in gaming and professional graphics applications. The GeForce 256 was a milestone not only for Nvidia but also for the entire technology industry, as it introduced a new standard for what graphics processors could achieve.

Beyond his technical contributions, Priem was also a driving force behind Nvidia's culture of innovation. His collaborative approach to problem-solving and his willingness to take risks on new ideas helped foster an environment at Nvidia where engineers were encouraged to push the limits of technology. This culture of innovation would become a hallmark of Nvidia's success, driving the company to continually lead the industry in graphics technology and beyond.

Priem's work at Nvidia also extended beyond the gaming and entertainment sectors. As the company grew, Nvidia's GPUs began to be used in a wide range of industries, from scientific research to automotive design. Priem's early contributions to Nvidia's product line helped lay the foundation for this diversification, as the GPUs he helped design were capable of handling the complex calculations required in fields like artificial intelligence, data science, and autonomous driving.

Today, Curtis Priem's legacy at Nvidia is still felt in the company's ongoing commitment to innovation in graphics processing and computing. Although he eventually stepped back from day-to-day operations at Nvidia, his influence remains a core part of the company's DNA. Nvidia's continued leadership in the tech industry is a testament to the vision and expertise that Priem brought to the company during its formative years.

Curtis Priem's journey from IBM to Sun Microsystems to Nvidia is a story of innovation, perseverance, and forward-thinking leadership. His work on some of the earliest graphics processors paved the way for the creation of Nvidia's groundbreaking GPUs, and his vision for the future of computing helped shape the company into the global leader it is today. As one of the key figures behind Nvidia's success, Priem's contributions to the tech industry have had a lasting impact, influencing not only the world of graphics but also the broader landscape of computing and technology.

The Convergence of Visionaries
The paths of Jensen Huang, Chris Malachowsky, and Curtis Priem converged in the early 1990s, a time when the tech industry was

undergoing rapid change. The rise of personal computing, the internet, and the increasing demand for multimedia experiences created a perfect storm of opportunity for these three visionaries. They shared a common belief that graphics processing would become a critical component of future computing, and they were determined to be at the forefront of this revolution.

In 1993, driven by their shared vision and complementary skills, Huang, Malachowsky, and Priem decided to strike out on their own and found a company that would focus on creating cutting-edge graphics technology. They named their company Nvidia, a name derived from the Latin word "invidia," meaning envy. The name was chosen to reflect the company's ambition to create technology that would inspire awe and admiration.

Together, Huang, Malachowsky, and Priem would lead Nvidia through its early challenges and successes, laying the foundation for what would become one of the most influential technology companies in the world.

The Birth of Nvidia
The founding of Nvidia in 1993 was a bold move by three engineers who saw an opportunity to revolutionize the world of computing through graphics processing. Jensen Huang, Chris Malachowsky, and Curtis Priem were united by a shared belief that the future of computing would be visual, and that graphics processing would become an essential component of all computing devices. However, turning this vision into reality would require overcoming significant challenges.

The Founding Vision
Nvidia was founded with a clear mission: to create a chip that could handle the complex computations required for 3D graphics. At the time, 3D graphics were in their infancy, with most computer

systems relying on 2D graphics for their visual output. The few systems that did support 3D graphics were expensive and often limited to specialized applications such as scientific visualization and high-end gaming.

Huang, Malachowsky, and Priem believed that 3D graphics would eventually become a mainstream technology, not just in gaming but in a wide range of applications, including professional visualization, entertainment, and even everyday computing tasks. They envisioned a future where 3D graphics would be an integral part of the computing experience, enabling richer, more immersive interactions between users and machines.

The founding team understood that achieving this vision would require creating a new kind of chip, one that could perform the complex mathematical calculations required for rendering 3D graphics quickly and efficiently. This chip would need to be powerful enough to handle the demands of 3D graphics, yet affordable enough to be integrated into a wide range of devices.

The Early Challenges
The early days of Nvidia were marked by significant challenges. The company was founded with limited resources, and the task of developing a groundbreaking new technology was daunting. Unlike established companies with large R&D budgets, Nvidia was a startup with a small team and a tight budget. Every decision had to be carefully considered, and the margin for error was slim.

One of the first challenges the team faced was securing funding. Developing a new chip was an expensive endeavor, and the founders knew they would need significant capital to bring their vision to life. Huang, who had a background in business as well as engineering, took the lead in seeking out investors who shared their belief in the potential of 3D graphics.

In the early 1990s, the tech industry was still reeling from the bursting of the PC bubble, and many investors were wary of putting money into hardware startups. Despite these challenges, Huang's passion and vision convinced several key investors to take a chance on Nvidia. Among the early investors were Sequoia Capital, a venture capital firm known for backing successful tech startups. Sequoia's investment was a vote of confidence in Nvidia's vision and provided the company with the initial capital it needed to begin development.

With funding secured, Nvidia began the process of designing its first product. The team knew that their success would depend on creating a chip that was not only powerful but also versatile enough to be used in a variety of applications. They set out to design a chip that could handle the demands of 3D graphics while also being efficient and cost-effective.

The Early Product Development
The first product that Nvidia developed was code-named NV1. The NV1 was a multimedia accelerator that combined 2D and 3D graphics, audio, and input/output functions into a single chip. This integration was a significant innovation at the time, as it allowed the chip to handle multiple types of data simultaneously, enabling richer and more immersive multimedia experiences.

Developing the NV1 was a complex and challenging process. The team had to overcome numerous technical hurdles, including how to efficiently render 3D graphics on a chip with limited processing power. One of the key innovations in the NV1 was the use of quadratic texture mapping, a technique that allowed the chip to render curved surfaces more realistically. This was a significant advancement over the flat, polygonal surfaces used in most 3D graphics at the time.

However, the NV1 faced several challenges in the market. One of the main issues was compatibility with existing software. At the time, most 3D games and applications were designed to use a different rendering method called polygonal texture mapping. Because the NV1 used a different rendering technique, it was not fully compatible with many popular games. This limited its appeal to consumers and developers, and the product did not achieve the commercial success the company had hoped for.

Despite the challenges, the development of the NV1 was a critical learning experience for Nvidia. It gave the team valuable insights into the complexities of graphics processing and helped them refine their approach to chip design. The NV1 also established Nvidia as a player in the graphics industry, laying the groundwork for future innovations.

Securing Initial Funding
Securing initial funding was one of the most critical steps in Nvidia's early journey. Without sufficient capital, the company would not have been able to develop its first products or bring its vision to market. Jensen Huang's leadership was instrumental in attracting investors who believed in the potential of 3D graphics.

In addition to Sequoia Capital, Nvidia attracted several other key investors in its early days. Among them was Sutter Hill Ventures, another prominent venture capital firm with a track record of investing in successful tech startups. The involvement of these high-profile investors provided Nvidia with the financial resources it needed to continue development and also gave the company credibility in the eyes of potential customers and partners.

Huang's ability to secure funding was a testament to his skills as a leader and communicator. He was able to articulate Nvidia's vision in a way that resonated with investors, convincing them that the company had the potential to revolutionize the computing industry. This ability to inspire confidence would become one of Huang's defining traits as he led Nvidia through its early challenges and into the future.

The Early Days

The early days of Nvidia were a period of intense innovation, experimentation, and learning. The company faced numerous challenges as it worked to develop its first products and establish itself in the competitive tech industry. Despite these challenges, Nvidia's founders remained committed to their vision, and their perseverance would eventually pay off.

Developing the First Products

After the launch of the NV1, Nvidia continued to refine its approach to graphics processing. The team recognized that the success of their products would depend on their ability to meet the needs of both developers and consumers. This meant not only creating powerful and versatile chips but also ensuring that their products were compatible with the software and applications that people were already using.

One of the key lessons Nvidia learned from the NV1 was the importance of industry standards. The NV1's compatibility issues had limited its market appeal, and the team was determined not to repeat this mistake. They began to focus on creating products that were compatible with the emerging standards in the graphics industry, including Microsoft's DirectX API, which was becoming the standard for 3D graphics in gaming and multimedia applications.

Nvidia's next major product was the RIVA 128, a graphics processing unit (GPU) that would become one of the company's first major successes. The RIVA 128 was designed to be fully compatible with DirectX, making it much more appealing to developers and consumers. It also featured improved performance and image quality, making it one of the most advanced graphics chips on the market at the time.

The RIVA 128 was a critical turning point for Nvidia. It established the company as a serious player in the graphics industry and helped it secure partnerships with major PC manufacturers. The success of the RIVA 128 also provided Nvidia with the financial resources it needed to continue developing new and innovative products.

Securing Initial Funding
Nvidia's early success would not have been possible without the financial backing of its investors. The funding provided by venture capital firms like Sequoia Capital and Sutter Hill Ventures allowed Nvidia to develop its first products, hire top talent, and establish itself in the industry.

In addition to venture capital, Nvidia also secured funding through strategic partnerships with other tech companies. For example, Nvidia partnered with SGS-Thomson Microelectronics (now STMicroelectronics) to manufacture its chips. This partnership provided Nvidia with access to the manufacturing capabilities it needed to produce its products at scale, while also giving the company additional financial resources.

These partnerships were critical to Nvidia's early success, as they allowed the company to focus on what it did best: developing cutting-edge technology. By leveraging the expertise and resources of its partners, Nvidia was able to bring its products to market more quickly and efficiently than it could have on its own.

Building the Team
Another key factor in Nvidia's early success was the strength of its team. From the beginning, Jensen Huang, Chris Malachowsky, and Curtis Priem were committed to building a team of top engineers who shared their passion for innovation and excellence. They understood that the success of their company would depend on the talent and dedication of the people who worked there.

Nvidia's founders were particularly focused on creating a culture of innovation and collaboration. They believed that the best ideas often came from the intersection of different perspectives and disciplines, and they encouraged their team to think creatively and take risks. This culture of innovation would become one of Nvidia's defining characteristics and would play a critical role in the company's future success.

In addition to technical expertise, Nvidia's founders also sought out individuals who were passionate about their work and committed to the company's vision. They understood that building a successful company required more than just technical skills; it also required a deep sense of purpose and a willingness to go above and beyond to achieve the company's goals.

Over time, Nvidia's team would grow to include some of the brightest minds in the tech industry. This talented and dedicated team would be instrumental in driving the company's growth and success in the years to come.

Overcoming Challenges
The early days of Nvidia were not without their challenges. The company faced intense competition from established players in the graphics industry, as well as the constant pressure to innovate and stay ahead of the curve. In addition, Nvidia had to navigate the

complex and rapidly changing landscape of the tech industry, where new technologies and trends could emerge at any time.

One of the key challenges Nvidia faced was the need to balance innovation with practicality. The company's founders were committed to pushing the boundaries of what was possible with graphics processing, but they also understood that their products needed to be practical and accessible to a wide range of users. This meant finding the right balance between cutting-edge technology and market demand.

Another challenge was managing the company's growth. As Nvidia began to achieve success with its products, it needed to scale its operations quickly to meet the increasing demand. This required careful planning and execution, as well as the ability to adapt to new challenges and opportunities as they arose.

Despite these challenges, Nvidia's founders remained committed to their vision and continued to push the company forward. Their perseverance and determination would eventually pay off, as Nvidia went on to become one of the most successful and influential technology companies in the world.

The founding of Nvidia in 1993 marked the beginning of a journey that would transform the world of computing and graphics. Driven by the vision and expertise of Jensen Huang, Chris Malachowsky, and Curtis Priem, Nvidia overcame significant challenges to develop its first products and establish itself as a leader in the tech industry.

The early days of Nvidia were a time of intense innovation and learning. The company faced numerous obstacles, but through determination, collaboration, and a relentless focus on its mission, Nvidia was able to achieve early success and lay the foundation for its future growth. The story of Nvidia's founding is a testament to the power of vision, innovation, and perseverance in the face of adversity.

Chapter 2:
The Graphics Revolution

The Creation of the GPU

The emergence of the Graphics Processing Unit (GPU) marked a transformative moment in the world of computing, redefining the way images and graphics are processed and rendered. The GPU's development was driven by the need for a specialized processor capable of handling the complex computations required for rendering high-quality 3D graphics, a task that traditional CPUs struggled to manage efficiently.

The Concept of the GPU

The concept of the GPU emerged from the realization that graphics processing required a different approach compared to general-purpose computing. Early computers used the Central Processing Unit (CPU) for all tasks, including graphics rendering. However, as graphics became more sophisticated, especially with the rise of 3D graphics, it became clear that CPUs were not optimized for these tasks.

In the early 1990s, the limitations of CPUs in handling the increasing demands of graphics rendering led to the idea of creating a dedicated processor designed specifically for this purpose. The goal was to develop a chip that could handle the complex mathematical calculations required for rendering 3D graphics, including transformations, lighting, and shading, more efficiently than a general-purpose CPU.

The concept of the GPU was driven by several key insights. First, graphics rendering involved a high degree of parallelism, where many calculations could be performed simultaneously. This parallelism was not well-suited to the sequential processing model of traditional CPUs. Second, the increasing complexity of graphics algorithms meant that a specialized processor could greatly enhance performance and enable new capabilities.

The idea of a dedicated graphics processor was not entirely new. Early graphics accelerators, such as those used in arcade games and early computer graphics systems, provided some level of specialized processing for graphics. However, these early accelerators were limited in their capabilities and were not designed to handle the full range of graphics computations required for modern 3D rendering.

The Development of the GPU

The development of the GPU was a complex and challenging process that required innovation in both hardware and software. The key challenge was designing a processor that could handle the specialized computations needed for 3D graphics while also being cost-effective and compatible with existing systems.

One of the pioneers in GPU development was Nvidia, a company founded by Jensen Huang, Chris Malachowsky, and Curtis Priem. Nvidia recognized the potential of a dedicated graphics processor and set out to create a chip that would revolutionize the world of graphics. The company's vision was to develop a processor that could handle the entire graphics pipeline, from vertex transformations to pixel shading, in a single chip.

The first step in developing the GPU was designing the architecture. Nvidia's team focused on creating a processor with a high degree of parallelism, capable of performing many calculations simultaneously. This required innovative approaches to chip design, including the use of multiple processing units and specialized hardware for different stages of the graphics pipeline.

One of the key innovations in the GPU's development was the use of programmable shaders. Shaders are small programs that define how graphics are rendered, including how vertices are transformed, how textures are applied, and how lighting and shading are calculated. Programmable shaders allowed developers to create custom effects and algorithms, greatly enhancing the flexibility and capabilities of the GPU.

The development of the GPU also required advances in memory architecture. Graphics processing involves the manipulation of large amounts of data, including textures, vertex data, and frame buffers. To handle these demands, the GPU needed a high-bandwidth memory system capable of transferring data quickly and efficiently.

Nvidia's team worked on developing a memory architecture that could support the high bandwidth requirements of modern graphics processing. This included the use of dedicated memory for the GPU, known as video memory or VRAM, which allowed the GPU to access and manipulate data quickly without relying on the system's main memory.

The creation of the GPU was a collaborative effort that involved contributions from many engineers and researchers. The development process included extensive testing and optimization to ensure that the GPU met the performance and compatibility requirements of modern graphics applications. The result was a new kind of processor that would fundamentally change the world of computing and graphics.

The Impact of the GPU
The introduction of the GPU had a profound impact on the computing industry. By providing a dedicated processor for graphics rendering, the GPU enabled significant improvements in

performance and image quality. It allowed for the development of more complex and realistic graphics, including detailed 3D environments, lifelike character animations, and advanced visual effects.

The GPU also paved the way for new applications and experiences. In gaming, the GPU enabled the creation of immersive 3D worlds with rich textures, dynamic lighting, and realistic physics. This revolutionized the gaming industry, leading to the development of more engaging and visually stunning games.

Beyond gaming, the GPU's capabilities extended to other areas, including professional visualization, scientific computing, and artificial intelligence. The ability to perform parallel computations made the GPU a powerful tool for tasks such as rendering complex simulations, analyzing large datasets, and training machine learning models.

The GPU's impact on the computing industry was not limited to performance and capabilities. It also influenced the development of new software and programming models. The introduction of programmable shaders and graphics APIs, such as DirectX and OpenGL, provided developers with new tools for creating advanced graphics and visual effects.

Overall, the creation of the GPU marked a major milestone in the evolution of computing technology. It demonstrated the power of specialized processors and paved the way for future innovations in graphics, visualization, and computation.

The GeForce 256

The GeForce 256, introduced by Nvidia in 1999, was a groundbreaking product that marked the debut of the world's first true GPU. Its release represented a significant leap forward in graphics technology, setting new standards for performance, image quality, and programmability.

The Concept of the GeForce 256
The GeForce 256 was designed to address the limitations of previous graphics accelerators and to push the boundaries of what was possible with computer graphics. Nvidia's goal was to create a graphics processor that could handle the full range of graphics computations required for modern 3D rendering, including vertex processing, texture mapping, and pixel shading.

One of the key innovations of the GeForce 256 was its ability to perform hardware-accelerated transform and lighting (T&L) calculations. T&L is a critical part of the graphics pipeline that involves transforming 3D vertices into screen space and calculating the lighting effects for each vertex. Prior to the GeForce 256, these calculations were performed by the CPU, which could be a bottleneck in achieving high-performance graphics.

The GeForce 256 incorporated dedicated hardware for T&L, allowing it to offload these computations from the CPU and handle them more efficiently. This innovation significantly improved performance and enabled more complex and detailed graphics in games and applications.

Another major feature of the GeForce 256 was its support for programmable shaders. Shaders are small programs that control various aspects of the rendering process, including how textures are applied, how lighting is calculated, and how visual effects are created. The GeForce 256 introduced support for programmable pixel shaders, allowing developers to create custom effects and algorithms that could be executed directly on the GPU.

The Impact of the GeForce 256 on the Gaming Industry

The GeForce 256 had a profound impact on the gaming industry, setting new standards for graphics performance and quality. Its support for hardware-accelerated T&L and programmable shaders allowed developers to create more realistic and immersive gaming experiences.

One of the most significant impacts of the GeForce 256 was its ability to deliver high-quality 3D graphics at a significantly lower cost than previous solutions. The GeForce 256's performance improvements allowed for more detailed textures, complex 3D environments, and advanced visual effects, all while keeping the price of the graphics card within reach of mainstream consumers.

The introduction of the GeForce 256 also spurred a wave of innovation in game development. Developers began to explore the possibilities of programmable shaders, creating new and exciting visual effects that were previously impossible or impractical. This led to a new generation of games with enhanced graphics, including more realistic lighting, dynamic shadows, and detailed character animations.

The GeForce 256's impact extended beyond gaming to other areas of computing. Its performance improvements and support for programmable shaders made it a valuable tool for professional visualization and digital content creation. Artists and designers used the GeForce 256 to create high-quality 3D models, animations, and visual effects, pushing the boundaries of what was possible in digital media.

The GeForce 256 in the Market

The GeForce 256 was a commercial success for Nvidia, establishing the company as a leader in the graphics industry. Its innovative features and performance capabilities set it apart from competing products, and it quickly gained popularity among gamers and professionals alike.

Nvidia's success with the GeForce 256 was also due in part to its strategic marketing and partnerships. The company worked closely with game developers to optimize their titles for the GeForce 256, ensuring that users could take full advantage of the card's capabilities. Nvidia also established strong relationships with PC manufacturers and retailers, ensuring that the GeForce 256 was widely available to consumers.

The GeForce 256's success laid the groundwork for Nvidia's future innovations in graphics technology. The card's introduction marked the beginning of a new era in graphics processing, where dedicated GPUs became the standard for high-performance computing. Nvidia continued to build on the success of the GeForce 256 with subsequent generations of GPUs, each one pushing the boundaries of graphics performance and capabilities.

The legacy of the GeForce 256 is evident in the continuing evolution of graphics technology. The innovations introduced with the GeForce 256, including hardware-accelerated T&L and programmable shaders, became foundational elements of modern GPUs. These features set the stage for future advancements in graphics processing, including the development of more advanced shader models, real-time ray tracing, and AI-powered graphics.

The GeForce 256 also had a lasting impact on the gaming industry, shaping the way games are developed and experienced. Its support for high-quality 3D graphics and programmable shaders allowed for the creation of more immersive and visually stunning games, influencing the direction of the industry for years to come.

Overall, the GeForce 256 represents a major milestone in the history of graphics technology. Its introduction marked the dawn of the GPU era and set a new standard for performance, image quality, and programmability. The innovations introduced with the GeForce 256 continue to influence the development of graphics technology, ensuring its place as a pivotal moment in the evolution of computing.

Dominating the Graphics Market

Nvidia's rise to dominance in the graphics market was marked by a series of strategic moves, innovative products, and a relentless focus on technology leadership. The company's success in establishing itself as the leader in graphics technology was driven by several key factors, including its commitment to innovation, strategic partnerships, and effective marketing.

Innovative Products and Technologies

Nvidia's success in the graphics market was largely due to its ability to deliver innovative products that set new standards for performance and capabilities. Following the success of the GeForce 256, Nvidia continued to push the boundaries of graphics technology with subsequent generations of GPUs.

One of the key innovations that helped Nvidia maintain its leadership position was the introduction of the GeForce2 series. The GeForce2 GPUs built on the success of the GeForce 256 by offering improved performance, higher clock speeds, and enhanced features. The GeForce2 GTS, for example, introduced support for hardware-accelerated transform and lighting, as well as higher memory bandwidth, further enhancing its performance and image quality.

Another major milestone in Nvidia's journey was the launch of the GeForce3 series, which introduced support for programmable vertex and pixel shaders. This allowed developers to create even more complex and detailed visual effects, further establishing Nvidia as a leader in graphics technology. The GeForce3's support for DirectX 8.0 and OpenGL 1.3 also ensured compatibility with the latest gaming and multimedia applications.

Nvidia's commitment to innovation continued with the introduction of the GeForce4 series, which featured advanced features such as shadow mapping and hardware support for anti-aliasing. The GeForce4 series further solidified Nvidia's position as the leader in graphics technology, providing gamers and professionals with cutting-edge performance and capabilities.

In addition to its focus on gaming, Nvidia also made significant strides in the professional graphics market. The company's Quadro series of GPUs, designed for professional visualization and CAD applications, provided high-performance graphics and advanced features for demanding users. The Quadro series helped Nvidia establish a strong presence in the professional market, complementing its success in gaming.

Strategic Partnerships and Collaborations
Nvidia's rise to dominance was also supported by strategic partnerships and collaborations with key players in the tech industry. The company worked closely with hardware manufacturers, game developers, and software vendors to ensure that its GPUs were compatible with a wide range of applications and systems.

One of the key partnerships that contributed to Nvidia's success was its collaboration with major PC manufacturers. By establishing strong relationships with companies such as Dell, HP, and IBM, Nvidia ensured that its GPUs were featured in a wide range of consumer and professional systems. This helped the company expand its market reach and increase its visibility among potential customers.

Nvidia also forged partnerships with leading game developers to optimize their titles for its GPUs. By working closely with developers, Nvidia was able to ensure that its GPUs delivered the best possible performance and visual quality for popular games. This helped the company build a strong reputation among gamers and establish itself as the go-to choice for high-performance graphics.

In addition to its partnerships with hardware and software vendors, Nvidia also collaborated with academic institutions and research organizations to advance the field of graphics technology. These collaborations helped Nvidia stay at the forefront of technological developments and contributed to the company's ability to deliver cutting-edge products.

Effective Marketing and Branding

Nvidia's dominance in the graphics market is not only a result of its technological innovations but also its highly effective marketing and branding strategies. By focusing on performance, building strong brand identities, and connecting with key audiences like gamers and professionals, Nvidia managed to solidify its place as a leader in the graphics industry.

One of the pillars of Nvidia's marketing strategy was its emphasis on product performance. Nvidia consistently highlighted the superior performance of its GPUs compared to competing products. The company backed up its claims with benchmark tests and real-world performance comparisons, which demonstrated the tangible advantages of its technology. This approach was particularly effective in capturing the attention of performance-driven customers, including gamers, creative professionals, and researchers who relied on high-powered graphics solutions. By focusing on speed, efficiency, and graphical quality, Nvidia positioned its GPUs as must-have components for anyone seeking top-tier performance, whether for gaming or professional applications.

The GeForce brand, aimed at gamers, and the Quadro brand, targeted at professionals in fields like design, engineering, and animation, became synonymous with cutting-edge technology. Nvidia's ability to clearly define its brands helped build customer trust and recognition. These products were marketed as industry-leading solutions in their respective categories, making it easier for consumers to choose Nvidia over competitors when looking for high-performance graphics. The strength of these brand identities, combined with the company's commitment to innovation, allowed Nvidia to establish itself as a key player not only in gaming but also in other areas like content creation and scientific computing.

Nvidia's branding extended to all facets of its marketing efforts, including product packaging, promotional materials, and advertisements. Each of these elements was designed to communicate Nvidia's core message of delivering advanced, high-quality graphics technology. The sleek, modern designs of its products, combined with an emphasis on power and innovation, created an image of a forward-thinking, technology-driven company. This consistent branding was a crucial part of Nvidia's success, helping the company stand out in a crowded marketplace.

Beyond traditional marketing, Nvidia capitalized on its connection with the gaming community, a crucial demographic for its GeForce brand. By sponsoring gaming events, competitions, and esports tournaments, Nvidia directly engaged with its target audience. This not only showcased the capabilities of its GPUs in real-world scenarios but also helped build loyalty among gamers. These events created opportunities for Nvidia to demonstrate the superior gaming experience made possible by its technology, from faster frame rates to enhanced visual effects. The company's involvement in gaming culture helped solidify its position as the go-to brand for serious gamers and positioned it as an integral part of the broader gaming ecosystem.

Esports, in particular, played a major role in Nvidia's marketing success. By sponsoring popular esports tournaments and teams, Nvidia connected with millions of gamers around the world. This exposure allowed the company to directly influence its target audience, many of whom placed a premium on performance when choosing hardware. Nvidia's presence in esports also reinforced the message that its GPUs were the best choice for competitive gaming, where even a small performance advantage could make the difference between victory and defeat.

Nvidia also invested in partnerships with game developers to optimize games for its GPUs. This strategy created a symbiotic relationship between Nvidia and the gaming industry, as developers worked to ensure their games ran best on Nvidia hardware, and Nvidia showcased these optimized games to highlight the capabilities of its products. This close collaboration helped position Nvidia as the default choice for gamers who wanted the best possible experience, driving demand for its GPUs.

By combining product performance with strong branding and strategic marketing efforts, Nvidia managed to not only dominate the graphics market but also build a loyal customer base across multiple industries. Whether through its gaming-focused GeForce line or its professional Quadro products, Nvidia's ability to market its GPUs as essential tools for achieving top performance played a significant role in its ongoing success.

Adapting to Market Trends

Nvidia's ability to adapt to changing market trends and technological advancements was another key factor in its dominance of the graphics market. The company continually evaluated emerging trends and technologies, adapting its product offerings and strategies to stay ahead of the competition.

One of the major trends that Nvidia capitalized on was the rise of high-definition and ultra-high-definition displays. As consumer demand for higher resolution displays increased, Nvidia developed GPUs with support for higher resolutions and enhanced image quality. This allowed the company to address the needs of both gamers and professionals who required high-resolution graphics for their applications.

Nvidia also embraced the growing importance of real-time ray tracing, a technology that simulates the behavior of light to create highly realistic images. The introduction of the RTX series of GPUs marked a major milestone in Nvidia's commitment to advancing graphics technology. The RTX series featured dedicated hardware for real-time ray tracing, enabling more realistic lighting, reflections, and shadows in games and applications.

In addition to its focus on real-time ray tracing, Nvidia also explored new areas of innovation, such as artificial intelligence and machine learning. The company's CUDA (Compute Unified Device Architecture) platform allowed developers to leverage the power of GPUs for a wide range of computational tasks beyond graphics, including data analysis, scientific simulations, and machine learning. This expansion into new areas helped Nvidia maintain its leadership position and drive growth in new markets.

Challenges and Competition

Despite its success, Nvidia faced significant challenges and competition throughout its journey to dominance in the graphics market. The company had to navigate a competitive landscape with rival companies such as AMD and Intel, each vying for market share in the graphics and computing industries.

One of the major challenges Nvidia faced was maintaining its technological leadership while managing the costs of research and development. The graphics market is highly competitive, with rapid advancements in technology and frequent product releases. Nvidia had to continuously innovate and invest in new technologies to stay ahead of its competitors.

Another challenge was addressing compatibility and performance issues across a wide range of systems and applications. As graphics technology evolved, Nvidia had to ensure that its products worked seamlessly with different hardware configurations, software environments, and operating systems.

Despite these challenges, Nvidia's focus on innovation, strategic partnerships, and effective marketing helped the company maintain its leadership position in the graphics market. The company's ability to adapt to changing trends and technologies allowed it to continue driving growth and success in a highly competitive industry.

Nvidia's rise to dominance in the graphics market is a testament to the company's commitment to innovation, strategic vision, and effective execution. The development of the GPU, the introduction of the GeForce 256, and the company's continued focus on cutting-edge technologies and market trends all contributed to its success.

The graphics revolution driven by Nvidia has had a profound impact on the computing industry, transforming the way graphics are rendered and experienced across a wide range of applications. From gaming to professional visualization, Nvidia's innovations have set new standards for performance, quality, and capabilities.

As Nvidia continues to lead the way in graphics technology, its legacy of innovation and excellence serves as an inspiration for the future of computing. The company's journey from its early days to its current position as a leader in the industry is a story of vision, perseverance, and technological advancement.

Chapter 3:
Expanding Beyond Graphics

Nvidia's Diversification Strategy

Nvidia's evolution from a specialized graphics company into a diversified technology powerhouse is a testament to its strategic vision and adaptability. While the company's initial success was rooted in its dominance in the graphics processing market, Nvidia's leadership recognized early on that relying solely on graphics technology would limit their growth potential. As a result, they embarked on a bold diversification strategy, expanding into professional visualization, data centers, and automotive industries. This strategy not only allowed Nvidia to tap into new markets but also to redefine its role in the technology landscape.

Expanding into Professional Visualization

Nvidia's venture into professional visualization marked a significant step in its expansion beyond consumer graphics, leveraging its expertise to meet the specific needs of industries like architecture, engineering, entertainment, and scientific research. The professional visualization market demands high-performance, precision, and reliability, especially for tasks that involve designing, modeling, and rendering complex visualizations. Recognizing this, Nvidia introduced its Quadro series of GPUs, tailor-made for professional environments.

The Quadro series set Nvidia apart in the professional graphics domain. These GPUs were designed with features that catered to the unique needs of professionals, offering enhanced precision, higher memory capacities, and support for advanced rendering techniques that surpassed what was available in consumer-grade GPUs. Quadro's architecture was built to ensure reliability in mission-critical tasks, making it the go-to choice for industries where precision and performance were non-negotiable.

In sectors like architecture and engineering, the demand for realistic and detailed 3D models has grown exponentially. Architects use software like AutoCAD, Revit, and SolidWorks to design buildings, infrastructure, and products, which require intensive computational power and graphical accuracy. Quadro GPUs became a critical tool in these industries, enabling professionals to visualize their projects with unmatched detail and accuracy. For instance, architects could generate high-fidelity renderings of buildings, complete with realistic lighting, materials, and environmental conditions, while engineers could simulate the structural integrity of their designs before any physical construction began.

Quadro GPUs' ability to process large datasets and handle complex simulations allowed users to create comprehensive visualizations of entire cities, bridges, and other infrastructure projects. This capability made them indispensable for architects and engineers working on massive projects, where real-time feedback on designs was crucial for making informed decisions. Additionally, the use of Quadro GPUs reduced the time it took to generate high-quality visuals, accelerating workflows and improving productivity.

Nvidia's influence extended heavily into the entertainment industry, particularly in the production of movies, television shows, and video games. The visual effects (VFX) industry, in particular, relies on advanced graphics processing to create the realistic and stunning effects seen in modern media. Quadro GPUs provided the computational horsepower needed to render the intricate visual effects used in blockbuster films, high-definition animations, and even virtual environments for video games.

For VFX artists and animators, the speed and precision of Quadro GPUs enabled the real-time rendering of complex scenes, allowing them to experiment with lighting, textures, and animations without waiting hours for their computers to process the changes. This led to more creative freedom and efficiency in the production pipeline. Films like Avatar and The Avengers employed Nvidia's Quadro GPUs to achieve the groundbreaking special effects that captivated audiences, demonstrating how essential these GPUs became in pushing the boundaries of cinematic experiences.

In addition to VFX, Quadro GPUs were also integral to the post-production process, including color correction, video editing, and compositing. The professional-grade GPUs allowed editors and colorists to work with high-resolution footage in real-time, ensuring that the final product met the highest standards of visual quality.

Nvidia's foray into scientific visualization is another area where its professional GPUs made a substantial impact. Researchers in fields such as biology, physics, and climate science often deal with vast amounts of data that require high-performance computing to visualize complex phenomena. For example, Quadro GPUs have been used in medical imaging to process and visualize detailed scans of human organs, helping doctors and researchers diagnose diseases and plan treatments more effectively.

In climate science, researchers use GPUs to simulate weather patterns, ocean currents, and the effects of climate change on a global scale. These simulations involve processing enormous datasets, and the ability of Nvidia's GPUs to handle this level of computational intensity allowed for more accurate and timely predictions. This has had far-reaching implications not just in academic research but in policy-making, where data-driven decisions about climate action and disaster preparedness are increasingly necessary.

Comprehensive Ecosystem: Hardware and Software Integration
Nvidia's approach to the professional visualization market didn't stop at developing powerful hardware. The company also focused on creating a comprehensive ecosystem of software, drivers, and development tools that optimized the performance of its GPUs across a wide range of professional applications. This included close partnerships with leading software developers in industries like architecture, engineering, media, and entertainment. By ensuring that Nvidia's GPUs were fully compatible and optimized for applications such as Autodesk Maya, Adobe Creative Suite, and Dassault Systèmes CATIA, Nvidia cemented its role as a trusted technology partner for professionals across various fields.

Moreover, Nvidia's proprietary software solutions, such as Nvidia RTX technology, introduced real-time ray tracing, a feature that enabled users to create more realistic lighting and shadows in their visualizations. This technology was revolutionary for industries that rely on visual accuracy, such as design and animation. Nvidia also introduced NVLink, a high-speed interconnect that allowed multiple GPUs to work together, significantly enhancing processing power for large-scale simulations and rendering tasks.

Another essential tool developed by Nvidia is the CUDA (Compute Unified Device Architecture) platform, which allows developers to use Nvidia's GPUs for parallel computing. CUDA became a game-changer not just in professional visualization but also in scientific research, artificial intelligence, and machine learning, as it allowed developers to harness the parallel processing power of GPUs for computational tasks that would have otherwise been handled by CPUs. This platform has been crucial in expanding the use of Nvidia's GPUs beyond graphics, contributing to the company's dominance in industries that require heavy data processing.

Venturing into Data Centers

The data center market represents a significant area of diversification for Nvidia, offering a new frontier beyond its traditional focus on graphics. Data centers serve as the backbone of modern digital infrastructure, providing businesses and organizations with the computational power and storage necessary to support applications like cloud computing, big data analytics, and online services. Nvidia's move into this space was driven by the growing demand for high-performance computing (HPC) solutions that can manage the ever-increasing volumes of data and the complexity of today's computing tasks.

Nvidia's entry into the data center market was a natural extension of its expertise in GPU technology. Traditional CPU-based data centers, while effective for general computing tasks, struggled to meet the demands of high-performance computing and large-scale data processing. Nvidia identified this gap and positioned its GPUs as a powerful alternative, offering parallel processing capabilities that could handle more demanding workloads. By leveraging its existing GPU technologies, Nvidia developed specialized solutions that went beyond the graphics space, focusing on the needs of data centers.

One of Nvidia's key innovations in this space was the development of the Tesla series of GPUs. Unlike consumer-grade GPUs, Tesla GPUs were designed specifically for high-performance computing environments. These GPUs provided the necessary computational power to accelerate tasks such as complex simulations, data analysis, and scientific computations. Their ability to process multiple tasks simultaneously allowed data centers to manage intensive workloads more efficiently, delivering faster results and enabling breakthroughs in fields such as scientific research, finance, and healthcare. This made Tesla GPUs a vital component in many high-performance computing setups.

Nvidia's GPUs also played a pivotal role in advancing artificial intelligence (AI) and deep learning within data centers. Machine learning and AI require enormous amounts of computational power to process and analyze vast datasets, and Nvidia's GPUs, with their parallel processing capabilities, were ideally suited for these tasks. Data centers equipped with Nvidia GPUs became the foundation for deploying machine learning models, performing complex image recognition, natural language processing, and predictive analytics. These advancements spurred growth in industries ranging from autonomous driving to healthcare diagnostics, demonstrating Nvidia's significant impact on the broader tech ecosystem.

Beyond hardware, Nvidia invested in developing the software platforms that would maximize the potential of its GPUs in data centers. The CUDA platform was a notable example of this effort, providing developers with tools and libraries to program Nvidia GPUs for a wide range of applications. CUDA allowed data scientists and engineers to take full advantage of the parallel processing power offered by Nvidia's hardware, enabling more efficient and scalable solutions for tasks like data analytics and machine learning. This software support made Nvidia's GPUs accessible and indispensable for a growing number of industries that rely on big data and AI.

Nvidia's strategic growth in the data center market was further bolstered by key acquisitions, such as its purchase of Mellanox Technologies in 2019. Mellanox was a leader in high-performance networking and interconnect solutions, technologies critical for connecting servers and enabling efficient data transfer within and between data centers. By acquiring Mellanox, Nvidia expanded its offerings beyond GPUs, delivering a more comprehensive solution for data center infrastructure that combined high-performance computing with robust networking capabilities. This move solidified Nvidia's position as a leading provider of end-to-end solutions for data centers, offering everything from processing power to advanced networking.

In summary, Nvidia's expansion into the data center market marked a major evolution in its business strategy. By developing high-performance GPU solutions like the Tesla series, advancing AI capabilities, and supporting these innovations with powerful software platforms like CUDA, Nvidia established itself as a key player in the data center industry. Strategic acquisitions like Mellanox further reinforced its presence, allowing Nvidia to deliver holistic solutions that meet the growing demands of data-driven industries. This diversification not only broadened Nvidia's market reach but also positioned the company as a leader in the future of computing infrastructure.

Entering the Automotive Sector

The automotive industry marks a third major area of diversification for Nvidia, aligning its advanced GPU technology with the evolving needs of modern vehicles. As the automotive landscape shifted toward incorporating cutting-edge electronics, connectivity, and automation, the demand for high-performance computing solutions surged. Technologies such as autonomous driving, infotainment systems, and advanced driver-assistance systems (ADAS) began to redefine the driving experience, and Nvidia recognized an opportunity to apply its expertise in graphics processing to this rapidly transforming industry.

Nvidia's strategic entry into the automotive sector was centered around the Nvidia DRIVE platform, a comprehensive suite of hardware and software solutions designed specifically for automotive applications. This platform offered manufacturers and developers the tools needed to integrate and deploy sophisticated computing systems within vehicles. One of the standout components of this platform was the DRIVE PX series, a family of automotive computers that integrate powerful GPUs alongside specialized processors. These computers were engineered to process real-time data from multiple sources such as sensors, cameras, and radar systems, allowing vehicles to make instantaneous decisions and navigate safely. The ability to handle vast amounts of data and run complex algorithms in real-time is crucial for the development of both autonomous vehicles and advanced ADAS features.

In addition to its hardware, Nvidia made significant investments in creating the software infrastructure necessary for automotive innovation. The DRIVE OS software stack became a key part of Nvidia's automotive offering. This unified operating system provided an integrated development environment for building automotive applications, ensuring that car manufacturers and developers could harness the full power of Nvidia's computing technology. With support for advanced algorithms, sensor fusion, and machine learning, DRIVE OS enabled the creation of sophisticated features like real-time object detection, vehicle-to-vehicle communication, and predictive decision-making systems for self-driving cars. The integration of machine learning was particularly valuable in advancing autonomous driving technologies, where continuous data analysis is required for complex tasks such as obstacle detection and route optimization.

Nvidia's focus on the automotive industry paid off as leading car manufacturers and technology firms adopted its solutions. Collaborations with top-tier automotive brands helped Nvidia establish itself as a crucial player in the industry's transformation toward smarter, safer vehicles. For example, partnerships with companies like Audi, Mercedes-Benz, and Tesla led to the deployment of Nvidia's GPUs in systems ranging from driver assistance to fully autonomous driving solutions. The company also worked with tier-one suppliers and technology partners to enhance infotainment systems, enabling immersive in-car experiences powered by Nvidia's graphics capabilities.

By positioning itself at the forefront of automotive innovation, Nvidia not only expanded its influence in an entirely new market but also contributed significantly to the advancement of next-generation vehicle technologies. The company's hardware and software solutions continue to drive developments in autonomous driving, ADAS, and in-vehicle infotainment, ensuring that Nvidia remains a central figure in shaping the future of transportation. This diversification into the automotive sector underscores Nvidia's ability to apply its core GPU technology across industries, transforming not just personal computing but also the future of mobility.

Nvidia's diversification strategy has allowed the company to expand beyond its origins in graphics technology and establish a presence in several high-growth markets. By venturing into professional visualization, data centers, and automotive applications, Nvidia has leveraged its expertise in GPU technology to drive innovation and growth across a range of industries. This strategic expansion has positioned Nvidia as a leader in multiple technology sectors and paved the way for future advancements in computing and visualization.

Entering the AI and Deep Learning Era
The transition to the era of artificial intelligence (AI) and deep learning represents one of the most significant developments in computing in recent years. Nvidia has played a central role in this transformation, leveraging its GPU technology to drive

advancements in machine learning, data analysis, and AI applications.

Leveraging GPUs for AI and Machine Learning

The rise of AI and deep learning has been intricately connected to the development of powerful computational resources that can handle the immense complexity of these technologies. Traditional CPUs, though versatile and effective for general-purpose computing, struggled to meet the unique demands of deep learning. This emerging field involves training neural networks with massive amounts of data and performing extensive parallel calculations, a process that quickly exceeds the capabilities of CPUs, which are optimized for sequential processing tasks. As AI models grew in size and complexity, researchers needed a solution that could handle the scale and performance demands required to push the boundaries of machine learning.

Nvidia's GPUs proved to be the answer. Known for their high degree of parallelism and raw computational power, GPUs were well-suited to tackle the specific challenges posed by deep learning workloads. Nvidia quickly recognized the potential of its GPU technology as a catalyst for AI and machine learning development and began to invest heavily in building solutions tailored for these advanced applications. The company's strategic foresight led to the transformation of its GPUs from graphics-focused processors to essential tools for the AI revolution.

One of the key factors that made GPUs ideal for AI and deep learning is their architecture, which is built to perform thousands of calculations simultaneously. Deep learning algorithms, especially neural networks, require extensive processing power because they involve adjusting millions, or even billions, of parameters. During the training process, neural networks learn from data by adjusting weights within the network, a task that requires computing large matrices of data and performing operations repeatedly across these matrices. GPUs, with their parallel processing architecture, can manage these vast computations much more efficiently than CPUs. This allows for faster training times, quicker iterations, and the ability to train more complex models, all of which are essential in the fast-evolving landscape of AI.

As AI research intensified, Nvidia's GPUs quickly became a staple within the AI and machine learning communities. Researchers and developers adopted Nvidia GPUs for a wide range of applications, including training deep neural networks, running inference on trained models, and conducting large-scale data analysis. One major advantage that GPUs brought to the table was the dramatic improvement in performance when compared to CPUs. Training deep learning models that would typically take weeks or months on a CPU could now be accomplished in a fraction of the time with Nvidia GPUs. This reduction in training time accelerated the development of new AI models, leading to faster innovation and more accurate outcomes across industries.

Beyond speed, Nvidia's GPUs offered a level of scalability that was critical for AI applications. As datasets grew in size and models became more complex, the computational demands increased exponentially. Nvidia's GPUs were designed to handle these larger workloads by leveraging their highly parallelized cores, making them ideal for processing the enormous datasets required for training deep learning models. This scalability enabled organizations to train models on massive datasets and deploy them in real-world applications such as autonomous vehicles, healthcare diagnostics, natural language processing, and recommendation systems, further cementing Nvidia's role as a leader in AI hardware.

Nvidia didn't stop at hardware. To fully unlock the potential of GPUs for AI and machine learning, the company developed software platforms like CUDA (Compute Unified Device Architecture). CUDA allowed developers to write software that could take full advantage of the parallelism in Nvidia's GPUs, making it easier to integrate GPUs into AI workflows. Nvidia also introduced specialized libraries such as cuDNN, which provided optimized functions for deep learning tasks, including convolutions and matrix multiplications—key operations in training neural networks. These software innovations played a pivotal role in expanding the accessibility and usability of GPUs for AI researchers, helping to standardize GPU-accelerated computing across the industry.

The combination of Nvidia's high-performance GPUs and its comprehensive software ecosystem has made it an indispensable player in the AI space. Its GPUs are now widely used in AI research and commercial applications, from autonomous driving and robotics to natural language processing and medical image analysis. By enabling faster and more efficient training of AI models, Nvidia's technology has helped unlock new possibilities for AI-driven innovations, positioning the company as a key enabler in the development of future AI technologies. As AI continues to evolve, Nvidia remains at the forefront, constantly pushing the boundaries of what is possible in the world of deep learning and artificial intelligence.

The Development of CUDA for AI

A pivotal element of Nvidia's strategy to bolster AI and deep learning was the creation of CUDA (Compute Unified Device Architecture). CUDA is a parallel computing platform and application programming interface (API) that transformed how developers approach general-purpose computing tasks. Initially designed for graphics processing, Nvidia's GPUs gained broader applicability with the introduction of CUDA, allowing them to be utilized in fields ranging from scientific research to machine learning and beyond. By providing developers with the tools to harness the immense parallel processing power of GPUs, CUDA bridged the gap between graphics computing and high-performance computing for AI applications.

The CUDA platform offered a new programming model that allowed developers to write software optimized for running on Nvidia GPUs. Its architecture enabled the efficient execution of parallel tasks, which is critical for applications requiring heavy computations, such as AI and deep learning. CUDA's design made it possible to leverage thousands of processing cores within Nvidia's GPUs, delivering far greater computational capacity than traditional CPUs, which rely on sequential processing. This advancement opened the door for developers to tackle problems that involve significant data and require high-speed calculations, such as training deep neural networks or running complex simulations.

The introduction of CUDA was a milestone for the AI community, significantly accelerating progress in the field. AI research, particularly deep learning, involves training models on vast datasets and performing numerous calculations to adjust network parameters. Before CUDA, AI researchers struggled with long training times and limited computational resources. CUDA-enabled GPUs transformed this landscape, offering an accessible way to scale these computations and reduce training times from weeks to days, or even hours, depending on the task. CUDA democratized access to high-performance computing, making it easier for researchers and developers to build cutting-edge AI applications without needing specialized hardware expertise.

One of CUDA's major strengths lies in its extensive library ecosystem, which includes tools, libraries, and frameworks specifically optimized for deep learning and AI workloads. CUDA provides libraries such as cuBLAS (for linear algebra), cuFFT (for Fourier transforms), and cuDNN (for deep learning operations), which optimize core mathematical functions essential for machine learning algorithms. These libraries greatly simplified the development process by offering pre-built, GPU-accelerated functions that developers could integrate into their AI models. This helped remove much of the complexity involved in building high-performance AI systems, allowing developers to focus on improving model architectures rather than dealing with low-level optimizations.

Nvidia also played a key role in supporting and optimizing popular deep learning frameworks for CUDA. Deep learning platforms such as TensorFlow, PyTorch, and Caffe became essential tools for developers working on AI projects. By integrating CUDA into these frameworks, Nvidia made it possible for developers to run their models more efficiently on Nvidia GPUs. This optimization led to substantial improvements in training times, allowing for faster iterations and experimentation, which in turn accelerated advancements in AI research and development. Nvidia's continuous updates to CUDA ensured that these frameworks could take advantage of the latest GPU innovations, further cementing Nvidia's leadership in the AI space.

In addition to deep learning, CUDA found applications in numerous other fields, including high-performance computing, scientific research, and data analytics. Researchers in fields like genomics, fluid dynamics, and financial modeling utilized CUDA to speed up complex calculations and simulations, making it a versatile tool far beyond its initial scope. This widespread adoption of CUDA across industries demonstrated the versatility and power of GPU acceleration, positioning Nvidia as a cornerstone of modern computing, especially in the context of AI and data-intensive tasks.

The impact of CUDA on AI and deep learning cannot be overstated. By offering a robust platform that maximized the potential of Nvidia's GPUs, CUDA became a foundational technology for the AI community. It empowered developers to build faster, more efficient models, pushing the boundaries of what AI systems could achieve. Through its continuous evolution, CUDA has remained at the heart of Nvidia's strategy, driving innovation across AI, deep learning, and a multitude of other industries where high-performance computing is essential.

The Impact of GPUs on AI Research and Development
Nvidia's GPUs have had a transformative impact on AI research and development, facilitating significant breakthroughs across diverse fields such as natural language processing (NLP), computer vision, and reinforcement learning. By providing the computational power necessary to train complex models, Nvidia's technology has been instrumental in enhancing the capabilities of AI systems and accelerating the pace of innovation in the sector.

In the realm of natural language processing (NLP), Nvidia's GPUs have played a crucial role in training large-scale language models, such as OpenAI's GPT-3. These models require immense computational resources to process and understand vast amounts of human language data effectively. Nvidia's GPUs enable researchers to handle the significant workloads associated with training these models, allowing them to develop state-of-the-art systems capable of performing a variety of tasks, including text generation, translation, and sentiment analysis. The efficiency and speed of GPU processing have made it possible for researchers to iterate quickly on model architectures and datasets, pushing the boundaries of what is possible in NLP.

In computer vision, Nvidia's GPUs have significantly advanced the development of sophisticated image recognition and object detection algorithms. These technologies are foundational for a multitude of applications, from powering autonomous vehicles to enhancing medical imaging techniques. With the ability to train deep neural networks that can accurately recognize and classify objects within images, Nvidia's GPUs have driven substantial advancements in areas such as autonomous driving, where vehicles need to interpret and respond to their surroundings in real time. Furthermore, in healthcare, AI systems powered by Nvidia GPUs have improved diagnostic accuracy through enhanced image analysis, allowing for better patient outcomes.

The field of reinforcement learning, which focuses on training agents to learn behaviors through interactions with their environments, has also seen significant benefits from Nvidia's GPU technology. The parallel processing capabilities of GPUs provide the necessary computational resources to train complex reinforcement learning algorithms efficiently. This has facilitated the development of systems that can learn intricate behaviors and strategies in various settings, leading to advancements in robotics, game playing, and optimization tasks. For instance, AI systems can now learn to navigate complex environments or play games at superhuman levels, demonstrating the profound impact of GPU technology on the advancement of intelligent systems.

In summary, Nvidia's GPUs have not only powered cutting-edge research in AI but have also enabled practical applications that are shaping the future of technology. By delivering the performance necessary to train large and complex models across multiple domains, Nvidia has positioned itself as a key player in the ongoing evolution of artificial intelligence. The company's ongoing commitment to innovation ensures that its GPUs will continue to facilitate groundbreaking developments in AI, helping researchers and developers tackle increasingly sophisticated challenges.

Nvidia's Contributions to AI Ecosystems
In addition to its hardware innovations, Nvidia has made significant strides in advancing the AI ecosystem through the development of comprehensive software platforms and tools tailored to meet the needs of researchers, developers, and organizations working in AI. By creating accessible frameworks and fostering collaboration within the AI community, Nvidia has helped accelerate progress and innovation in artificial intelligence.

One of the most impactful software contributions from Nvidia is the Nvidia Deep Learning AI (DLA) framework. DLA is a robust, scalable, and highly efficient framework specifically designed to support the deployment of AI models on Nvidia GPUs. With built-in capabilities for training, inference, and model optimization, DLA allows developers to build and implement AI solutions with ease while taking full advantage of the computational power of Nvidia's GPUs. This framework streamlines the process of deploying high-performance AI models, reducing the complexity and cost associated with scaling AI solutions in real-world environments. By offering support for various stages of AI development, from initial training to real-time inference, Nvidia's DLA framework is a vital tool for organizations seeking to implement cutting-edge AI applications across industries.

Beyond the tools themselves, Nvidia has also played a critical role in promoting collaboration and knowledge sharing within the AI community. The company actively organizes and hosts the Nvidia GPU Technology Conference (GTC), an influential global event where researchers, developers, and industry leaders come together to discuss advancements in AI, deep learning, and GPU technologies. At GTC, participants have the opportunity to learn from Nvidia's experts, engage in hands-on labs, and explore the latest breakthroughs in AI research and applications. By providing a platform for knowledge exchange and fostering connections between different stakeholders in the AI field, Nvidia's GTC has become an important driver of innovation and growth within the AI ecosystem.

Additionally, Nvidia supports the integration of its software tools into widely used AI development frameworks, including TensorFlow, PyTorch, and Caffe. By ensuring that these frameworks are optimized for Nvidia's GPU architecture, the company has made it easier for AI researchers and engineers to leverage GPU acceleration for training and inference tasks. This integration has been instrumental in accelerating the development of AI applications, enabling faster training times, higher accuracy, and more efficient resource utilization.

Through its combination of advanced hardware, powerful software tools, and community-building initiatives, Nvidia has positioned itself as a key enabler of AI progress. By supporting AI developers and researchers with both the infrastructure and platforms needed to push the boundaries of what is possible, Nvidia continues to play a vital role in shaping the future of artificial intelligence.

Nvidia's entry into the AI and deep learning era represents a pivotal moment in the company's evolution. By leveraging its GPU technology to accelerate AI and machine learning workloads, Nvidia has played a central role in driving advancements in the field. The development of CUDA, the impact of GPUs on AI research, and Nvidia's contributions to the AI ecosystem have all contributed to the company's success in this rapidly growing market. As AI continues to evolve, Nvidia's technology and innovations will remain at the forefront of driving progress and shaping the future of computing.

The Rise of CUDA

The introduction of CUDA (Compute Unified Device Architecture) marked a significant turning point in the history of computing, transforming how developers and researchers harness the power of Nvidia's GPUs for a wide range of applications. CUDA represents one of Nvidia's most impactful innovations, enabling general-purpose computing on GPUs and driving advancements in various fields, from scientific research to machine learning and beyond.

The concept of CUDA emerged from Nvidia's desire to unlock the full potential of its GPUs beyond traditional graphics processing. While GPUs were initially designed for rendering graphics, their parallel processing architecture proved to be highly effective for other types of computations. Nvidia recognized that GPUs could be used for general-purpose computing tasks, such as scientific simulations, data analysis, and machine learning, if developers had the right tools and programming model.

CUDA was introduced in 2006 as a parallel computing platform and API that allowed developers to write software that could run on Nvidia's GPUs. The goal of CUDA was to provide a programming model that would make it easier for developers to leverage the power of GPUs for tasks beyond graphics rendering. CUDA aimed to bridge the gap between traditional CPU-based computing and the parallel processing capabilities of GPUs.

The CUDA Programming Model

The CUDA programming model is based on the concept of parallel computing, where tasks are divided into smaller sub-tasks that can be executed simultaneously. This model takes advantage of the massive parallelism of GPUs, which can perform thousands of calculations concurrently.

In CUDA, computations are organized into threads, blocks, and grids. Threads are the smallest units of execution, and multiple threads are grouped together into blocks. Blocks are then organized into grids, creating a hierarchical structure that allows for scalable parallelism. This model enables developers to write programs that can efficiently utilize the resources of Nvidia's GPUs.

The CUDA programming model also provides support for memory management, allowing developers to allocate and manage memory on the GPU. This includes global memory, shared memory, and local memory, each with different characteristics and usage scenarios. Efficient memory management is crucial for achieving optimal performance in CUDA programs.

CUDA and General-Purpose Computing
CUDA has had a profound impact on general-purpose computing, enabling a wide range of applications that benefit from GPU acceleration. One of the key areas where CUDA has made a significant impact is scientific computing. Researchers in fields such as physics, chemistry, and biology have used CUDA to accelerate simulations, data analysis, and modeling tasks. CUDA has allowed scientists to tackle complex problems that require substantial computational power, leading to advancements in areas such as molecular dynamics, fluid dynamics, and climate modeling.

In addition to scientific computing, CUDA has been widely adopted in the field of data analytics. The ability to process large volumes of data quickly and efficiently has made CUDA a valuable tool for data scientists and analysts. CUDA has been used to accelerate tasks such as data processing, statistical analysis, and machine learning, enabling faster insights and more accurate results.

Machine learning and deep learning have also benefited significantly from CUDA. Training deep neural networks involves performing numerous calculations in parallel, making GPUs an ideal platform for this task. CUDA has enabled researchers and developers to build and train complex machine learning models more efficiently, leading to advancements in areas such as computer vision, natural language processing, and reinforcement learning.

The Ecosystem of CUDA

The success of CUDA can be attributed in part to the ecosystem of tools, libraries, and frameworks that support its use. Nvidia has developed a range of software tools and libraries to facilitate CUDA development and optimize performance.

One of the key tools in the CUDA ecosystem is the CUDA Toolkit, which provides a comprehensive set of development tools, libraries, and documentation. The toolkit includes the CUDA compiler (nvcc), profiling and debugging tools, and libraries for various tasks, such as linear algebra (cuBLAS) and Fourier transforms (cuFFT). The toolkit also includes support for popular programming languages such as C, C++, and Fortran.

Nvidia has also developed a range of libraries and frameworks that leverage CUDA for specific applications. For example, cuDNN (CUDA Deep Neural Network library) provides optimized implementations of deep learning operations, such as convolution and activation functions, for use with deep learning frameworks. Similarly, cuSPARSE provides optimized routines for sparse matrix operations, which are commonly used in scientific computing and machine learning.

The CUDA ecosystem extends beyond Nvidia's own tools and libraries. Many popular third-party libraries and frameworks have been optimized for CUDA, allowing developers to take advantage of GPU acceleration in their applications. For example, deep learning frameworks such as TensorFlow, PyTorch, and Keras have integrated support for CUDA, enabling researchers and developers to leverage the power of GPUs for training and deploying machine learning models.

The Impact of CUDA on Innovation

The introduction of CUDA has had a profound impact on innovation in computing, enabling new applications and driving advancements in various fields. By providing a programming model that makes it easier to harness the power of GPUs, CUDA has opened up new possibilities for researchers, developers, and businesses.

In scientific research, CUDA has enabled breakthroughs in fields such as genomics, astrophysics, and materials science. Researchers have used CUDA to accelerate simulations and data analysis, leading to new discoveries and insights. For example, CUDA has been used to simulate the behavior of complex biological systems, model the formation of galaxies, and study the properties of materials at the atomic scale.

In industry, CUDA has driven innovations in areas such as finance, healthcare, and manufacturing. For example, in finance, CUDA has been used to accelerate risk modeling and portfolio optimization, leading to more accurate and timely financial decisions. In healthcare, CUDA has enabled advancements in medical imaging, such as faster and more accurate image reconstruction and analysis. In manufacturing, CUDA has been used to optimize production processes and improve quality control.

The Future of CUDA

As computing continues to evolve, CUDA is likely to remain a key technology for leveraging the power of GPUs. Nvidia continues to invest in CUDA and develop new features and capabilities to support emerging applications and trends.

One of the key areas of focus for the future of CUDA is the integration of GPUs with other types of processing units, such as CPUs and specialized accelerators. The growing complexity of computing tasks and the need for heterogeneous computing environments are driving the development of new architectures and programming models. CUDA is expected to play a role in these developments, providing support for new types of computing systems and applications.

Another area of focus for CUDA is the continued optimization of performance and efficiency. Nvidia is constantly working to improve the performance of its GPUs and the efficiency of CUDA programs. This includes advancements in hardware design, such as the introduction of new GPU architectures, as well as improvements in software tools and libraries.

The rise of CUDA represents one of the most significant advancements in computing, enabling general-purpose computing on Nvidia's GPUs and driving innovation across a wide range of fields. By providing a powerful programming model and a comprehensive ecosystem of tools and libraries, CUDA has transformed how developers and researchers harness the power of GPUs for applications beyond graphics.

The impact of CUDA on scientific research, data analytics, machine learning, and other areas has been profound, leading to new discoveries and advancements in various fields. As computing continues to evolve, CUDA is likely to remain a key technology, driving innovation and shaping the future of computing. Nvidia's commitment to CUDA and its ongoing development reflects the company's dedication to advancing technology and supporting the needs of its users.

Chapter 4:
Innovations and Acquisitions

Key Innovations in GPU Technology

Nvidia has been a leader in graphics technology and computing innovation, consistently pushing the boundaries of what's possible with its GPUs. Over the years, the company has introduced several groundbreaking technologies that have transformed various industries. Key innovations include Ray Tracing, Tensor Cores, and Deep Learning Super Sampling (DLSS). These technologies have not only advanced graphics rendering but also enabled new applications in fields such as artificial intelligence and machine learning.

Ray Tracing

Ray tracing is a rendering technique that simulates the behavior of light in a way that mirrors how it interacts with objects in the real world, leading to incredibly lifelike visuals. Unlike traditional rasterization methods, which approximate lighting effects and often rely on tricks to simulate realism, ray tracing tracks the actual paths of individual rays of light as they travel through a scene, interact with surfaces, reflect off objects, and refract through transparent materials. This method enables much more accurate rendering of phenomena like reflections, refractions, and shadows, resulting in images that closely resemble real-world lighting conditions.

Although ray tracing has been around for decades, its computational demands historically made it impractical for real-time applications, especially in gaming. The sheer complexity of simulating thousands or even millions of light rays bouncing off multiple surfaces in a scene meant that ray tracing was reserved for industries like film and animation, where rendering could take hours or days per frame. However, Nvidia's introduction of dedicated ray tracing hardware in its Turing architecture fundamentally changed this landscape. With the launch of the GeForce RTX 20 series GPUs, Nvidia unveiled RT Cores, specialized processors designed to accelerate ray tracing computations, making real-time ray tracing a reality for gaming and interactive applications.

The inclusion of RT Cores in the RTX 20 series allowed for real-time ray tracing in games and other interactive environments. These cores handle the computationally intensive task of tracing light rays and calculating how they interact with objects, dramatically improving performance. As a result, developers could finally incorporate ray tracing into video games without sacrificing performance. For the first time, players could experience dynamic, realistic lighting effects, such as true-to-life reflections on surfaces like water and glass, detailed shadows that behave realistically depending on the light source, and more accurate refractions through transparent objects.

This breakthrough has had a profound impact on the gaming industry. Games that incorporate ray tracing technology are able to deliver unprecedented levels of visual realism, making environments feel more immersive and dynamic. Games like "Cyberpunk 2077," "Control," and "Shadow of the Tomb Raider" serve as prime examples of how ray tracing can elevate the graphical experience, showcasing realistic lighting, shadowing, and reflections that would have been impossible to achieve in real time using traditional techniques. These titles not only demonstrate the visual potential of ray tracing but also set a new standard for gaming graphics moving forward.

By enabling developers to harness real-time ray tracing, Nvidia has pushed the boundaries of what is visually possible in gaming, paving the way for more immersive and visually stunning experiences. As the technology continues to evolve and become more widely adopted, it is likely to play a central role in shaping the future of gaming and interactive media.

Tensor Cores

Tensor Cores, introduced by Nvidia with the Volta architecture and further refined in subsequent generations, represent a major leap forward in accelerating deep learning and machine learning tasks. Unlike traditional CUDA cores, which are designed for general-purpose computing, Tensor Cores are specialized units optimized for performing tensor operations, which are essential for the mathematical computations involved in neural network training and inference. These operations primarily involve matrix multiplications, a core process in deep learning algorithms that Tensor Cores are uniquely equipped to handle.

One of the most significant benefits of Tensor Cores is their ability to perform mixed-precision matrix calculations. In traditional GPU cores, higher-precision calculations (like 32-bit floating-point operations) are standard, but these can be computationally expensive and slower when dealing with the massive datasets required for deep learning. Tensor Cores, by contrast, use mixed-precision—combining 16-bit and 32-bit operations—which allows them to perform complex calculations with reduced precision without sacrificing accuracy, enabling faster computation. This efficient handling of data allows AI models to train much more quickly and makes the use of Tensor Cores a key feature in high-performance AI systems.

The introduction of Tensor Cores has significantly impacted various industries by enhancing the performance of AI and machine learning applications. In the field of artificial intelligence, Tensor Cores have reduced the time required to train deep learning models, enabling researchers and developers to work with larger datasets and more complex algorithms. This acceleration has led to breakthroughs in natural language processing (NLP), where models like GPT and BERT can process vast amounts of text data faster and more efficiently. Similarly, image recognition systems have benefited from Tensor Cores' ability to accelerate the training of convolutional neural networks (CNNs), making applications such as autonomous vehicles, medical imaging, and facial recognition more reliable and effective.

In addition to improving training times, Tensor Cores have also enhanced inference performance, the process where trained models make predictions or classifications. This has facilitated real-time applications such as speech recognition, object detection, and natural language translation, bringing sophisticated AI capabilities to consumer products, industrial solutions, and research labs alike. By enabling faster model training and inference, Tensor Cores have paved the way for more sophisticated AI algorithms, allowing industries to push the boundaries of what's possible in fields like robotics, autonomous systems, and intelligent automation.

As AI continues to evolve, Nvidia's Tensor Cores remain a cornerstone in driving advancements in the field, offering unparalleled performance improvements and expanding the possibilities for innovation across sectors reliant on AI-driven technologies.

Deep Learning Super Sampling (DLSS)

Deep Learning Super Sampling (DLSS), introduced by Nvidia with the RTX 20 series GPUs, represents a groundbreaking application of AI and machine learning in gaming. Designed to enhance both performance and image quality, DLSS leverages neural networks to upscale lower-resolution images to higher resolutions, allowing for better performance without compromising visual fidelity. By offloading some of the graphical computation to AI-driven processes, DLSS offers a solution to the inherent trade-off between high frame rates and stunning visuals, a common challenge in gaming and other graphically intensive applications.

The core mechanism of DLSS involves training a neural network on a dataset of high-resolution images. The network learns to predict the appearance of higher-resolution frames based on low-resolution input. During gameplay, the DLSS algorithm uses this pre-trained neural network to upscale the rendered lower-resolution frames, transforming them into images that appear as if they were rendered natively at a higher resolution. This process allows the game to run at a lower resolution, which requires less computational power, while still delivering high-quality, visually impressive scenes.

For gamers, the primary benefit of DLSS is the ability to achieve higher frame rates and smoother gameplay while maintaining crisp and detailed visuals. This is particularly important for graphically demanding titles, where running the game at native 4K resolution, for example, would put significant strain on even the most powerful hardware. DLSS effectively lightens the load on the GPU, allowing it to maintain a higher level of performance. Games like "Control," "Cyberpunk 2077," and "Metro Exodus" have demonstrated how DLSS can dramatically improve both performance and visual quality, making the gaming experience more immersive and fluid.

Each iteration of DLSS has seen improvements. DLSS 2.0, for instance, brought significant refinements in image quality, achieving near-native or even better-than-native results in some cases. By further optimizing the neural networks and adding support for a broader range of resolutions and hardware configurations, Nvidia continues to enhance DLSS with each update. The most recent versions, such as DLSS 3, also introduce frame generation capabilities, where AI not only upscales images but also creates entirely new frames, further improving performance in supported titles.

Beyond gaming, the impact of DLSS extends into other fields like virtual reality (VR) and professional visualization. In VR, where high frame rates and low latency are crucial for a seamless and immersive experience, DLSS helps deliver these demanding performance requirements while maintaining high visual fidelity. Similarly, in industries such as architecture, engineering, and product design, where professionals rely on real-time visualization and high-quality rendering, DLSS provides the necessary performance boost to handle large models and complex environments without sacrificing detail.

In summary, DLSS is a transformative technology that combines the power of AI with cutting-edge graphics to enhance both performance and visual quality. Whether it's enabling higher frame rates in the latest AAA games or pushing the boundaries of virtual reality and professional rendering, DLSS showcases the growing role of AI-driven innovation in graphics and real-time computation..

Nvidia's innovations in GPU technology, including Ray Tracing, Tensor Cores, and DLSS, have had a transformative impact on various industries. These technologies have advanced graphics rendering, accelerated AI and machine learning workloads, and enhanced gaming performance. As Nvidia continues to push the boundaries of GPU technology, it is likely that new innovations will further shape the future of computing and digital experiences.

Strategic Acquisitions

Nvidia's growth and success are not only attributed to its technological innovations but also to its strategic acquisitions. By acquiring companies with complementary technologies and expertise, Nvidia has expanded its capabilities and strengthened its position in key markets. Notable acquisitions include Mellanox Technologies and ARM Holdings, each of which has had a significant impact on Nvidia's business strategy and industry presence.

Mellanox Technologies

Mellanox Technologies, a prominent provider of high-performance networking solutions, was acquired by Nvidia in 2019 for $6.9 billion. This acquisition marked a significant strategic move for Nvidia, which aimed to enhance its data center offerings and meet the rising demand for high-speed networking solutions. Mellanox specialized in products like InfiniBand and Ethernet adapters, switches, and software, all designed to improve data center performance and connectivity.

Integrating Mellanox's technology into Nvidia's ecosystem allowed for the creation of an end-to-end solution that encompassed both computing and networking components. This combination was particularly beneficial for high-performance computing (HPC) and artificial intelligence (AI) applications, as it provided a seamless interface between GPUs and networking infrastructure. One of the standout features of Mellanox's technology is its InfiniBand solution, which is renowned for its low latency and high throughput. This capability is crucial for data-intensive workloads, where rapid and efficient communication between GPUs and other system components is essential for optimal performance.

The acquisition also served to bolster Nvidia's presence in the data center market, facilitating stronger relationships with major cloud service providers and enterprise customers. By offering a complete portfolio of data center solutions that include both high-performance computing capabilities and advanced networking technology, Nvidia positioned itself as a leader in the HPC market. This strategic alignment not only enhanced Nvidia's competitive edge but also catered to the evolving needs of businesses and organizations that require sophisticated computing and networking solutions.

Furthermore, the integration of Mellanox's technology has allowed Nvidia to offer comprehensive solutions that address various industry challenges, from managing massive data workloads to optimizing network performance in complex data centers. As organizations increasingly rely on data-driven decision-making and high-speed computing, the synergy between Nvidia's GPUs and Mellanox's networking solutions plays a pivotal role in delivering the performance and efficiency required to stay competitive in today's fast-paced technological landscape.

ARM Holdings
In September 2020, Nvidia announced plans to acquire ARM Holdings, a leader in semiconductor intellectual property (IP), in a deal valued at $40 billion. ARM's technology powers a vast array of devices, including mobile phones, embedded systems, and other electronic applications, making it a highly valuable asset for Nvidia's ambitious growth strategy. ARM's architecture underpins a significant portion of the global tech landscape, from smartphones to Internet of Things (IoT) devices, so the acquisition promised substantial implications for both companies and the wider tech industry.

Nvidia's strategic goal with the ARM acquisition was to leverage ARM's CPU designs and expertise in low-power processing to complement its own GPU and AI technologies. The acquisition would allow Nvidia to broaden its reach beyond traditional markets such as gaming and high-performance computing (HPC) into new sectors like mobile computing, IoT, and edge computing. ARM's semiconductor designs are renowned for their power efficiency, which made them a natural fit for Nvidia's strategy to deliver high-performance, energy-efficient solutions across a broader range of applications.

One of the major potential advantages of the deal was the integration of ARM's CPU designs with Nvidia's GPUs and AI platforms. By combining ARM's low-power processors with Nvidia's expertise in AI, machine learning, and graphics, Nvidia hoped to deliver innovative solutions in areas such as autonomous vehicles, data centers, and smart devices. For example, in the realm of automotive technology, Nvidia's AI-driven software could be paired with ARM's energy-efficient CPUs to create more intelligent, responsive systems for self-driving cars.

The acquisition also positioned Nvidia to play a larger role in the semiconductor industry, giving it access to ARM's vast ecosystem of partners, which includes major players across the technology spectrum. ARM's intellectual property is licensed to many of the world's leading semiconductor companies, providing Nvidia with new opportunities for collaboration and innovation. This move signaled Nvidia's broader ambitions to shape the development of next-generation technologies, including influencing future hardware standards and semiconductor designs.

However, the proposed acquisition faced significant regulatory hurdles. Regulatory bodies in the US, UK, European Union, and China expressed concerns over how the acquisition might affect competition and innovation in the global semiconductor industry. Critics feared that Nvidia's control over ARM could disrupt the neutrality ARM had historically maintained in its licensing model, potentially stifling competition in industries where ARM's designs are widely used. Key stakeholders, including Google, Microsoft, and Qualcomm, voiced concerns that the deal might harm ARM's neutral licensing practices and inhibit innovation.

As of early 2024, the acquisition remained under regulatory review, with uncertainty surrounding its final approval. If approved, the acquisition would undoubtedly reshape the semiconductor landscape and accelerate Nvidia's strategic push into emerging markets. On the other hand, should it be blocked, Nvidia would need to seek alternative ways to expand its footprint in sectors like mobile computing and IoT. Regardless of the outcome, the acquisition of ARM by Nvidia was poised to have significant and lasting effects on the tech industry, influencing everything from smartphones to AI-driven infrastructure.

Nvidia's strategic acquisitions of Mellanox Technologies and ARM Holdings have played a crucial role in the company's growth and diversification. These acquisitions have allowed Nvidia to expand its capabilities, enhance its product offerings, and strengthen its position in key markets. As Nvidia continues to pursue strategic opportunities, its acquisitions are likely to shape the company's future and influence the technology industry as a whole.

Impact on Various Industries
Nvidia's innovations and acquisitions have had a profound impact on several industries, including gaming, artificial intelligence, automotive, and healthcare. By pushing the boundaries of technology and expanding into new markets, Nvidia has influenced the development and advancement of various applications and solutions.

Gaming

Nvidia's innovations in GPU technology, including Ray Tracing, Tensor Cores, and DLSS, have revolutionized the gaming industry. These technologies have enhanced the visual quality of games, improved performance, and provided new experiences for gamers.

Ray Tracing has brought a new level of realism to gaming graphics, allowing developers to create more lifelike environments and lighting effects. The introduction of RTX graphics cards and dedicated RT Cores has enabled real-time ray tracing, resulting in games with accurate reflections, shadows, and lighting. Titles such as "Cyberpunk 2077" and "Control" showcase the impact of ray tracing, delivering visually stunning experiences that push the boundaries of gaming graphics.

DLSS has also played a significant role in improving gaming performance. By using AI and machine learning to upscale lower-resolution images, DLSS allows games to run at higher frame rates while maintaining visual quality. This technology has been particularly beneficial for gamers with high-resolution displays and demanding games, providing smoother gameplay and better overall performance.

Nvidia's innovations have not only improved the quality of gaming but also driven advancements in game development. Game developers now have access to powerful tools and technologies that enable them to create more immersive and visually impressive games. The integration of Nvidia's technologies into game engines and development workflows has led to new possibilities for game design and storytelling.

Artificial Intelligence

Nvidia's impact on artificial intelligence (AI) has been profound, with the company's GPUs and CUDA technology driving advancements in machine learning, deep learning, and data analytics. Tensor Cores, in particular, have accelerated AI and machine learning workloads, enabling researchers and developers to build and train complex models more efficiently.

The use of GPUs for AI research and development has led to significant breakthroughs in various fields, including natural language processing, image recognition, and reinforcement learning. Nvidia's contributions to the AI ecosystem, including the development of frameworks such as CUDA and libraries like cuDNN, have facilitated the growth of AI applications and research.

Nvidia's AI technologies have also influenced industries beyond research. In healthcare, AI-powered medical imaging and diagnostics have improved the accuracy and speed of disease detection and treatment. In finance, AI algorithms have been used for risk modeling and portfolio optimization, leading to more informed financial decisions. The integration of Nvidia's GPUs into data centers and cloud platforms has enabled businesses to leverage AI for a wide range of applications, from predictive analytics to autonomous systems.

Automotive

Nvidia's expansion into the automotive industry has been driven by its expertise in GPU technology and AI. The company's automotive solutions include platforms for advanced driver assistance systems (ADAS), autonomous driving, and in-car entertainment.

Nvidia's Drive platform is a comprehensive suite of hardware and software solutions designed to support autonomous driving and ADAS. The platform includes GPUs, AI processors, and development tools that enable automotive manufacturers to build and deploy advanced driver assistance systems and self-driving vehicles. Nvidia's Drive AGX system-on-a-chip (SoC) provides the computational power required for real-time processing of sensor data and decision-making in autonomous vehicles.

The integration of Nvidia's technology into automotive systems has led to advancements in safety, convenience, and user experience. Features such as lane-keeping assistance, adaptive cruise control, and automated parking are powered by Nvidia's AI and GPU technology, providing drivers with enhanced safety and convenience.

Nvidia's automotive solutions also extend to in-car entertainment and infotainment systems. The company's technology enables high-quality graphics and multimedia experiences for passengers, including advanced navigation, gaming, and streaming services. Nvidia's collaboration with automotive manufacturers and technology partners has driven innovation in automotive electronics and user experience.

Healthcare
Nvidia's impact on healthcare has been driven by its advancements in AI and GPU technology. The company's GPUs and AI frameworks have enabled new applications in medical imaging, genomics, and drug discovery.

In medical imaging, Nvidia's GPUs have accelerated the processing and analysis of medical images, leading to faster and more accurate diagnostics. AI algorithms powered by Nvidia's technology have been used to improve image reconstruction, detection, and segmentation, enhancing the ability of radiologists to identify and diagnose conditions.

Nvidia's contributions to genomics and drug discovery include the use of GPUs for high-performance computing tasks such as genome sequencing and molecular modeling. The company's technology has enabled researchers to analyze large-scale genomic data and simulate the behavior of biological molecules, leading to advancements in personalized medicine and drug development.

The integration of Nvidia's AI and GPU technology into healthcare applications has also supported the development of new tools for patient monitoring, treatment planning, and clinical research. Nvidia's collaboration with healthcare providers and researchers has driven innovation in medical technology and improved patient outcomes.

Nvidia's innovations and acquisitions have had a transformative impact on various industries, including gaming, artificial intelligence, automotive, and healthcare. By advancing GPU technology and expanding into new markets, Nvidia has influenced the development of cutting-edge applications and solutions that drive progress and improve experiences across multiple sectors. As Nvidia continues to innovate and explore new opportunities, its contributions are likely to shape the future of technology and its applications in diverse fields.

Chapter 5:
Challenges and Controversies

Navigating Industry Competition

Nvidia has been a dominant force in the graphics processing unit (GPU) market, but its journey has been fraught with intense competition. The company has had to navigate challenges from formidable rivals such as Advanced Micro Devices (AMD) and Intel. These competitors have pushed Nvidia to continuously innovate and adapt to changing market dynamics, influencing the evolution of the GPU industry.

Competition from AMD

Advanced Micro Devices (AMD) has long been one of Nvidia's most formidable competitors in the GPU market, fostering a rivalry that has driven innovation and advancement in the graphics industry. AMD's journey into the GPU space began with its 2006 acquisition of ATI Technologies, a strategic move that gave AMD a robust presence in the graphics industry and positioned it as a significant competitor to Nvidia's dominance. Since then, the competition between the two companies has intensified, resulting in a series of technological battles and market shifts.

AMD's Radeon graphics cards have consistently challenged Nvidia's GeForce lineup. The competition between the Radeon and GeForce brands has been marked by a back-and-forth contest to deliver superior performance, advanced features, and better value to consumers. This fierce rivalry has accelerated the pace of GPU innovation, with each company pushing the limits of what their technology can achieve. For instance, AMD's Radeon RX series, based on the RDNA architecture, was a clear demonstration of the company's commitment to offering high-performance gaming solutions at competitive prices, directly competing with Nvidia's products in terms of both power and affordability.

One pivotal moment in this ongoing competition occurred in 2019, when AMD launched the Radeon RX 5000 series. Based on the RDNA architecture, this series was designed to compete aggressively with Nvidia's mid-range and high-end GPUs, a segment where Nvidia had enjoyed significant dominance. AMD's Radeon RX 5000 series offered impressive performance at lower price points, disrupting Nvidia's market position and forcing the company to respond. The RX 5700 XT, in particular, stood out as a strong competitor, delivering high-end gaming performance and challenging Nvidia's GeForce RTX 2060 and 2070 offerings.

In response, Nvidia launched the GeForce RTX 20 series, powered by the Turing architecture. This series introduced groundbreaking features like real-time ray tracing and Deep Learning Super Sampling (DLSS), which elevated visual fidelity and gaming performance to new heights. The inclusion of RT Cores for ray tracing and Tensor Cores for AI-driven enhancements gave Nvidia a technological edge in graphics realism. This marked a significant milestone in the rivalry, as AMD had yet to fully implement ray tracing into their GPUs, allowing Nvidia to temporarily take the lead in delivering cutting-edge gaming experiences.

However, AMD quickly adapted, incorporating ray tracing in its subsequent Radeon RX 6000 series with the RDNA 2 architecture, further heating up the competition. AMD's ability to close the technological gap with Nvidia and continue offering competitive pricing reinforced the importance of this rivalry in pushing both companies to stay at the forefront of GPU advancements.

The rivalry between AMD and Nvidia extends beyond just consumer gaming GPUs. Both companies have expanded into areas such as professional visualization, data centers, and high-performance computing (HPC), offering solutions that cater to industries like artificial intelligence, machine learning, and deep learning. Nvidia's Tesla and Quadro GPUs have long been popular choices for professionals working in these fields, providing the necessary computational power for AI training and large-scale simulations. In response, AMD has developed its own lineup of Radeon Pro GPUs and EPYC processors, making substantial inroads in the professional and enterprise markets.

In the data center and cloud computing space, AMD's EPYC processors have gained a reputation for delivering excellent performance, especially in combination with the Radeon Instinct GPUs, which are optimized for machine learning and AI workloads. AMD's aggressive moves in the data center market have positioned it as a strong competitor to Nvidia, which remains dominant with its A100 GPUs based on the Ampere architecture, designed for intensive AI and HPC applications.

Overall, the rivalry between AMD and Nvidia has been pivotal in driving GPU innovation, spurring advancements in gaming, AI, machine learning, and data center technologies. This competitive dynamic has not only benefited consumers by offering a wider range of powerful and affordable GPUs but has also shaped the future of computational graphics and AI research. As both companies continue to evolve their technologies, the ongoing competition promises to fuel further breakthroughs in the years to come.

Competition from Intel

Intel, long recognized for its dominance in the central processing unit (CPU) market, has taken significant steps into the graphics processing unit (GPU) sector, adding a new dimension to Nvidia's competitive landscape. Intel's strategic entry into the GPU market began with the development of its discrete graphics solutions under the Xe brand, marking a bold move to compete with established players like Nvidia and AMD.

The introduction of Intel's Xe GPUs represents a pivotal shift in the industry. Unlike its historical focus on integrated graphics, Intel is now expanding into discrete GPU technologies with ambitions to compete across multiple market segments. The Xe architecture is structured to address a wide range of needs, from integrated graphics for everyday users to high-performance computing (HPC) for enterprise applications. The architecture is divided into three primary categories: Xe-LP (Low Power) for integrated and entry-level graphics, Xe-HPG (High-Performance Gaming) for gaming and discrete GPUs, and Xe-HPC for data centers and HPC workloads.

One of Intel's key milestones was the launch of Intel Iris Xe Graphics in 2020. This integrated GPU aimed to challenge mid-range offerings from both AMD and Nvidia, delivering enhanced graphics performance for laptops, consumer applications, and professional use cases. With the Xe-LP architecture, Intel demonstrated its intent to provide competitive solutions in the integrated graphics segment, an area historically dominated by AMD's Radeon Vega and Nvidia's MX series.

However, Intel's ambitions extended beyond integrated solutions. In 2021, the company introduced its first discrete GPUs under the Xe-HPG (High-Performance Gaming) architecture, marking its formal entry into the discrete GPU market. Designed to compete directly with Nvidia's GeForce RTX series and AMD's Radeon RX series, Xe-HPG GPUs offer advanced features like hardware-accelerated ray tracing, variable-rate shading, and AI-driven supersampling, positioning Intel as a new contender in the gaming space. This foray into high-performance gaming GPUs signaled Intel's determination to challenge Nvidia's long-standing dominance in the gaming and enthusiast markets.

Intel's development of Xe-HPC architecture further extended its reach into data centers and HPC applications, where Nvidia has a strong presence with its Ampere and Hopper architectures. Xe-HPC is designed for AI, machine learning, and scientific computing, offering massive computational power aimed at workloads that demand fast, efficient processing. This development reflects Intel's strategy to target a broader range of applications beyond consumer graphics, entering the AI and data center markets where Nvidia has historically been a leader.

The competition between Intel and Nvidia is not confined to the consumer and gaming markets. As both companies expand into sectors like data centers, cloud computing, and artificial intelligence (AI), their rivalry has intensified. Intel's focus on GPU development has spurred Nvidia to continue pushing the boundaries of innovation. For example, Nvidia's rapid advancements in AI frameworks, deep learning accelerators, and HPC solutions have been essential in maintaining its market leadership, especially as Intel seeks to disrupt Nvidia's hold on the data center GPU market with Xe-HPC.

As Intel continues to evolve its GPU technology, the competition among the three giants—Intel, Nvidia, and AMD—promises to drive further advancements in GPU design, performance, and features. The dynamic nature of the GPU market ensures that these companies remain locked in a cycle of technological innovation, where each new product launch redefines the competitive landscape and sets new standards for performance across gaming, professional visualization, and AI applications.

Adapting to Market Dynamics

The competition from AMD and Intel has required Nvidia to adapt and evolve its strategies to maintain its leadership position. The company has focused on several key areas to address competitive pressures:

Technological Innovation: Nvidia has consistently invested in research and development to drive technological advancements. Innovations such as ray tracing, DLSS, and Tensor Cores have set Nvidia's products apart from competitors and provided a competitive advantage.

Product Diversification: Nvidia has expanded its product portfolio beyond consumer graphics cards to include solutions for professional visualization, data centers, and automotive applications. This diversification has allowed Nvidia to tap into new markets and reduce reliance on any single segment.

Strategic Partnerships: Nvidia has formed strategic partnerships with various industry players to enhance its market position. Collaborations with game developers, cloud service providers, and automotive manufacturers have helped Nvidia integrate its technologies into a wide range of applications.

Pricing and Positioning: Nvidia has employed strategic pricing and positioning to address competitive threats. By offering a range of products with varying performance levels and price points, Nvidia has catered to different segments of the market and responded to competitive pressures.

The competition from AMD and Intel has driven Nvidia to continuously innovate and adapt to changing market conditions. The dynamic nature of the GPU industry ensures that competition remains a central factor in shaping the company's strategies and technological advancements.

Legal Battles and Patent Disputes

As a leading technology company, Nvidia has faced several legal challenges and patent disputes over the years. These legal battles have involved issues related to intellectual property, antitrust regulations, and competition with other technology firms. Navigating these legal challenges has been an important aspect of Nvidia's business strategy and has had implications for its operations and market positioning.

Patent Disputes

Nvidia has faced several significant patent disputes over the years, particularly related to its GPU technology and innovations. These disputes often center around intellectual property rights, with claims of patent infringement either brought by Nvidia against competitors or vice versa. The high-stakes nature of these legal battles underscores the competitive landscape of the GPU industry and the critical importance of protecting technological advancements.

One of the most notable disputes was a legal confrontation with AMD in 2017. Nvidia initiated a lawsuit against AMD, alleging that AMD's graphics processing units (GPUs) infringed on patents held by Nvidia, particularly concerning GPU architecture and memory management technologies. Nvidia argued that certain aspects of AMD's GPUs were based on proprietary technologies that Nvidia had developed and patented. Although the specific terms were not made public, the case was ultimately settled with an undisclosed agreement, highlighting the significance of intellectual property protection in the competitive battle for market dominance.

Another important legal battle in the same year involved a lawsuit against Qualcomm, where Nvidia accused the mobile chip giant of patent infringement. The case centered on claims that Qualcomm had used Nvidia's patented technologies related to graphics processing and mobile technology in its chipsets without authorization. Similar to the case with AMD, the dispute was resolved through a licensing agreement, allowing both companies to continue utilizing their respective technologies while resolving the issue outside the courtroom. This licensing agreement signaled a cooperative resolution in a rapidly evolving mobile technology market, where graphics performance plays an increasingly crucial role.

Aside from disputes initiated by Nvidia, the company has also been forced to defend its own patents against allegations of infringement. For example, Nvidia has had to protect its proprietary innovations in GPU design, architecture, and computational technologies from competitors and other entities seeking to challenge its intellectual property claims. These legal defenses are crucial for maintaining the company's competitive edge in the industry, as its innovative advancements—ranging from ray tracing to AI-enhanced graphics—are key differentiators that drive its success.

Overall, these patent disputes illustrate the complex legal environment surrounding the tech industry, where companies must be vigilant in defending their intellectual property while navigating challenges from competitors. For Nvidia, staying ahead of the curve in terms of technological innovation and securing patents for those advancements has been a central part of maintaining its leadership in the GPU market. At the same time, negotiating settlements and licensing agreements allows for a balance between legal enforcement and ongoing technological development.

Antitrust Regulations
Nvidia has encountered antitrust scrutiny from regulators due to its growing market dominance and competitive practices,

particularly in sectors like GPUs, AI, and data centers. These investigations have focused on whether Nvidia's business strategies align with competition laws and whether they could potentially harm consumers or stifle competition in various markets.

One of the most significant antitrust investigations emerged from Nvidia's acquisition of Mellanox Technologies in 2019. Mellanox, a leader in high-performance networking solutions, became a key piece in Nvidia's strategy to expand its data center business. However, this $6.9 billion acquisition raised concerns among regulators such as the U.S. Federal Trade Commission (FTC) and the European Commission. These regulatory bodies scrutinized the deal to determine whether it would reduce competition, drive up prices, or stifle innovation in the data center market.

The review process involved a detailed assessment of the potential competitive effects of the acquisition, including how it might impact competitors in networking technologies like InfiniBand and Ethernet solutions. Mellanox's dominant position in these markets raised questions about Nvidia's control over both computing and networking infrastructure in data centers, particularly for cloud service providers and enterprise customers. Despite these concerns, the acquisition was ultimately approved by regulatory authorities after they were convinced it would not significantly harm competition, though the process highlighted the regulatory challenges Nvidia faces as it continues to grow through strategic acquisitions.

Beyond acquisitions, Nvidia's broader business practices have drawn scrutiny in relation to its market influence over GPU pricing, distribution, and supply chains. The company's near-duopoly with AMD in the graphics card market has led regulators to closely monitor Nvidia's pricing strategies and whether its dominant position might harm competition or limit consumer choices. With its deep involvement in emerging technologies like AI and high-performance computing (HPC), Nvidia's growing market share has made it a target for antitrust investigations across multiple jurisdictions.

Compliance and Settlements
To navigate these legal challenges, Nvidia has adopted a range of strategies aimed at resolving disputes efficiently while ensuring business continuity. One of the most common approaches has been the use of settlements and licensing agreements. These arrangements allow Nvidia to address legal challenges without engaging in lengthy litigation that could disrupt its operations or damage its reputation.

In some instances, Nvidia has reached settlements with competitors over patent disputes, enabling both parties to avoid prolonged legal battles. These settlements typically involve financial compensation or mutual agreements to cease certain practices. For example, Nvidia's patent lawsuits against AMD and Qualcomm were resolved through settlements, allowing the parties to move forward without further legal escalation.

Nvidia has also used licensing agreements as a strategic tool to resolve disputes while maintaining control over its intellectual property. These agreements allow other companies to use Nvidia's technologies, typically in exchange for royalties or other financial terms, while protecting Nvidia's innovations from infringement. Licensing arrangements also enable Nvidia to foster collaborative relationships within the industry, particularly in sectors like AI, machine learning, and automotive technologies, where partnerships can drive new growth opportunities.

Strategic Implications

Nvidia's efforts to address legal challenges and comply with competition laws have become a crucial aspect of its broader business strategy. As the company expands into new markets and industries, particularly through acquisitions, regulatory scrutiny is likely to remain a significant consideration. The ability to navigate these challenges effectively, through a combination of compliance, settlements, and strategic partnerships, has helped Nvidia maintain its competitive edge and position itself as a leader in the tech landscape.

By staying ahead of legal and regulatory issues, Nvidia ensures that it can continue innovating and expanding without being hindered by legal roadblocks. However, the growing importance of intellectual property protection and regulatory compliance means that Nvidia must remain vigilant and proactive in addressing these challenges as it solidifies its leadership in critical markets like AI, data centers, and GPUs.

Nvidia's legal battles and patent disputes have been a significant aspect of the company's business landscape. The challenges related to intellectual property, antitrust regulations, and competition with other technology firms have required Nvidia to navigate complex legal issues and protect its innovations. As Nvidia continues to grow and evolve, addressing legal challenges and maintaining compliance with regulations will remain important considerations for the company's success.

The ARM Acquisition Controversy

The attempted acquisition of ARM Holdings by Nvidia was one of the most high-profile and controversial moves in the company's history. Announced in September 2020, the $40 billion acquisition aimed to expand Nvidia's reach into new markets and leverage ARM's semiconductor intellectual property (IP) for a wide range of applications. However, the acquisition faced significant scrutiny and challenges from regulators, competitors, and industry stakeholders.

ARM Holdings, headquartered in Cambridge, UK, is a leading designer of semiconductor IP, including CPU and GPU architectures used in a wide range of devices. ARM's technology is integral to mobile devices, embedded systems, and other applications, making it a valuable asset for Nvidia's growth strategy.

The acquisition was intended to enhance Nvidia's product offerings and expand its presence in markets beyond graphics processing. ARM's extensive portfolio of IP provided Nvidia with the opportunity to integrate advanced CPU and GPU designs into its solutions, targeting new segments such as mobile computing, Internet of Things (IoT), and edge computing.

The acquisition was also seen as a strategic move to position Nvidia as a more prominent player in the semiconductor industry. By acquiring ARM, Nvidia aimed to influence the development of future technologies and standards, leveraging ARM's ecosystem of partners and licensees.

Regulatory Scrutiny and Challenges
The ARM acquisition faced intense regulatory scrutiny from authorities around the world. The review process involved assessments by antitrust regulators and competition authorities in various jurisdictions, including the U.S., the European Union, and the UK.

1. Antitrust Concerns
Regulators expressed concerns about the potential anti-competitive effects of the acquisition. The primary issue was whether Nvidia's acquisition of ARM would lead to reduced competition in the semiconductor market and harm competitors.

Concerns were raised about Nvidia's ability to leverage ARM's IP to gain an unfair advantage and limit access for other companies.

The U.S. Federal Trade Commission (FTC) conducted a thorough review of the acquisition, examining the potential impact on competition in the semiconductor industry. The European Commission and the UK Competition and Markets Authority (CMA) also conducted investigations to assess the competitive effects of the deal.

2. Industry Opposition

The acquisition faced opposition from various industry stakeholders, including competitors, customers, and technology advocates. Some industry players expressed concerns about Nvidia's intentions and the potential impact on ARM's business model and ecosystem.

Competitors such as Intel and AMD voiced apprehension about Nvidia's increased influence over semiconductor technology. Customers who relied on ARM's IP for their products were concerned about potential changes in licensing terms and access to technology.

3. Geopolitical Considerations

The acquisition also encountered geopolitical challenges. Given ARM's UK-based headquarters, the acquisition faced scrutiny from UK regulators and government officials. The UK government expressed concerns about the implications of the deal for national security and technology sovereignty.

Outcome and Impact

In February 2022, Nvidia announced that it had officially terminated the acquisition of ARM due to regulatory hurdles and opposition. The decision marked the end of a high-profile deal that had faced significant challenges and uncertainties.

The termination of the acquisition had several implications for Nvidia and the semiconductor industry. Nvidia's focus shifted back to its core business of GPU technology and data centers, while ARM remained an independent entity. The acquisition controversy highlighted the complexities of large-scale mergers and acquisitions in the technology sector and the importance of regulatory compliance.

The ARM acquisition controversy was a significant chapter in Nvidia's history, reflecting the challenges and complexities associated with large-scale mergers and acquisitions. The regulatory scrutiny, industry opposition, and geopolitical considerations underscored the importance of addressing competitive and strategic issues in the semiconductor industry. As Nvidia continues to navigate the evolving technology landscape, the experience from the ARM acquisition will likely influence its future strategies and approaches to growth.

Chapter 6:
Nvidia's Role in the AI Revolution

The AI Renaissance

The rise of artificial intelligence (AI) has marked one of the most transformative periods in technological history. Central to this AI renaissance has been Nvidia, whose GPUs have played a pivotal role in accelerating AI development and deployment across various industries. This chapter explores how Nvidia's GPUs became integral to the AI revolution, reshaping the landscape of technology and innovation.

The Emergence of AI and Deep Learning

Artificial intelligence, particularly deep learning, has experienced a resurgence in recent years, driven by advances in computational power, data availability, and algorithmic innovations. Deep learning, a subset of machine learning, involves training neural networks with multiple layers to perform tasks such as image recognition, natural language processing, and autonomous decision-making.

The success of deep learning algorithms hinges on the ability to process vast amounts of data and perform complex calculations quickly. Traditional CPUs, while powerful for general computing tasks, were not optimized for the parallel processing required by deep learning models. This challenge led to a growing demand for specialized hardware capable of handling the intense computational requirements of AI workloads.

Nvidia's GPUs and Parallel Processing

Nvidia's Graphics Processing Units (GPUs) emerged as a game-changer in the AI field due to their parallel processing capabilities. Unlike CPUs, which are designed for sequential processing tasks, GPUs are engineered to handle multiple tasks simultaneously. This parallel architecture makes GPUs exceptionally well-suited for the matrix and vector operations central to deep learning.

The introduction of Nvidia's CUDA (Compute Unified Device Architecture) in 2006 was a milestone in this context. CUDA provided a programming model and API that allowed developers to harness the power of GPUs for general-purpose computing tasks beyond graphics rendering. This innovation enabled researchers and engineers to accelerate AI training and inference tasks using Nvidia's GPUs, revolutionizing the way deep learning models were developed and deployed.

Key Developments in GPU Technology
Nvidia's commitment to advancing GPU technology has played a crucial role in supporting the AI revolution. The company's GPU architectures, such as the Tesla, Kepler, Maxwell, Pascal, Volta, and Turing series, have introduced various enhancements that have significantly impacted AI research and applications.

Tesla Architecture: The Tesla architecture, introduced in 2006, marked Nvidia's entry into high-performance computing with GPUs optimized for parallel processing. Tesla GPUs laid the groundwork for future developments in AI acceleration.

Kepler Architecture: The Kepler architecture, launched in 2012, introduced significant improvements in energy efficiency and performance. The architecture included features like dynamic parallelism and Hyper-Q, which enhanced the ability to handle complex AI workloads.

Maxwell Architecture: Maxwell, introduced in 2014, brought advancements in performance and power efficiency. The architecture's improved compute capability and memory bandwidth contributed to faster training and inference times for deep learning models.

Pascal Architecture: The Pascal architecture, unveiled in 2016, introduced the high-bandwidth memory (HBM2) and NVLink interconnect technology. These innovations provided a substantial boost in memory bandwidth and data transfer rates, further accelerating AI computations.

Volta Architecture: The Volta architecture, launched in 2017, featured Tensor Cores specifically designed for deep learning operations. Tensor Cores provided significant performance improvements for matrix multiplications, a core operation in many AI algorithms.

Turing Architecture: The Turing architecture, introduced in 2018, included advancements such as real-time ray tracing and AI-enhanced graphics. Turing GPUs also featured enhanced Tensor Cores and support for AI-driven applications.

Impact on AI Research and Development
Nvidia's GPUs have had a profound impact on AI research and development. The ability to accelerate deep learning model training has enabled researchers to explore more complex models and datasets, leading to breakthroughs in various AI applications. Key areas of impact include:

Natural Language Processing (NLP): GPUs have accelerated the training of large language models, such as GPT-3 and BERT, which have revolutionized natural language understanding and generation. These models have enabled advancements in chatbots, language translation, and text analysis.

Computer Vision: GPUs have facilitated the development of advanced computer vision algorithms used in image recognition, object detection, and image segmentation. These advancements have applications in autonomous vehicles, medical imaging, and surveillance.

Reinforcement Learning: GPUs have supported the training of reinforcement learning algorithms used in robotics, gaming, and autonomous systems. The ability to perform simulations and training in parallel has accelerated the development of intelligent agents capable of complex decision-making.

Generative Models: GPUs have enabled the training of generative models, such as Generative Adversarial Networks (GANs), which are used for creating realistic images, videos, and audio. These models have applications in creative industries, content generation, and data augmentation.

Collaborations and Ecosystem Development
Nvidia's role in the AI revolution extends beyond hardware development to include fostering a vibrant ecosystem of developers, researchers, and partners. The company has invested in creating tools, frameworks, and platforms that support AI innovation.

Developer Tools and Libraries: Nvidia provides a range of developer tools and libraries that simplify AI development and deployment. These include CUDA, cuDNN (CUDA Deep Neural Network library), and TensorRT (Nvidia Tensor Runtime). These tools enhance the performance and efficiency of deep learning frameworks and applications.

AI Research Partnerships: Nvidia has collaborated with leading research institutions and universities to advance AI research. These partnerships have led to the development of new algorithms, models, and applications that push the boundaries of AI capabilities.

AI Competitions and Challenges: Nvidia has sponsored and supported AI competitions and challenges that encourage innovation and collaboration within the AI community. These events provide opportunities for researchers and developers to showcase their work and contribute to the advancement of AI technology.

Nvidia's GPUs have become central to the AI renaissance, enabling the rapid development and deployment of deep learning models and applications. The company's commitment to advancing GPU technology and supporting the AI ecosystem has positioned Nvidia as a key player in the AI revolution. As AI continues to evolve, Nvidia's contributions will remain instrumental in shaping the future of technology and innovation.

Nvidia's AI Platforms

Nvidia has developed a range of AI platforms that leverage its GPU technology to address various challenges and opportunities across industries. These platforms, including Nvidia DGX, Clara, and Jarvis, provide comprehensive solutions for AI development, deployment, and application. This section explores the introduction and impact of these platforms in transforming industries and driving innovation.

Nvidia DGX

Nvidia DGX is a series of high-performance computing platforms designed to accelerate AI and deep learning workloads. The DGX systems are built on Nvidia's GPU technology and provide a complete hardware and software solution for training and deploying AI models.

The Nvidia DGX platform was first introduced in 2016 with the launch of the DGX-1. The DGX-1 was designed to provide a turnkey solution for AI research and development, featuring multiple Nvidia GPUs, high-speed interconnects, and pre-installed AI software.

Key features of Nvidia DGX systems include:

High-Performance GPUs: DGX systems are equipped with Nvidia's latest GPUs, including Tesla V100 and A100 GPUs. These GPUs provide exceptional performance for deep learning and AI workloads, with high memory bandwidth and processing power.

NVLink Interconnect: DGX systems use Nvidia's NVLink technology to enable high-speed communication between GPUs. NVLink provides a unified memory space and low-latency data transfers, enhancing the performance of distributed AI training.

Optimized Software Stack: DGX systems come with a pre-installed software stack that includes Nvidia's CUDA, cuDNN, and TensorRT libraries. The software stack is optimized for Nvidia's GPUs and provides a seamless development environment for AI applications.

Scalability: DGX systems are designed for scalability, allowing users to connect multiple DGX units to create a high-performance AI cluster. This scalability supports large-scale AI training and inference tasks.

Nvidia DGX systems have had a significant impact on AI research and development by providing researchers and organizations with powerful tools for accelerating their work. The platform has facilitated advancements in various areas of AI:

Deep Learning Model Training: DGX systems have enabled researchers to train large and complex deep learning models more efficiently. The high-performance GPUs and optimized software stack reduce training times and improve model accuracy.

AI Research and Innovation: The availability of DGX systems has accelerated the pace of AI research and innovation. Researchers can experiment with new algorithms, architectures, and datasets, leading to breakthroughs in fields such as natural language processing, computer vision, and reinforcement learning.

Enterprise AI Adoption: DGX systems have supported enterprises in adopting AI technologies by providing a turnkey solution for developing and deploying AI applications. Organizations in various industries, including finance, healthcare, and manufacturing, have leveraged DGX systems to drive AI-driven insights and solutions.

Nvidia Clara
Nvidia Clara is a platform designed to accelerate AI and high-performance computing applications in healthcare and life sciences. The platform provides a range of tools and solutions for medical imaging, genomics, and drug discovery.

Nvidia Clara was introduced in 2018 and aims to address the unique challenges of healthcare and life sciences through AI and computational power. Key features of the Clara platform include:

Medical Imaging Solutions: Clara provides AI-powered tools for medical imaging, including image reconstruction, segmentation, and analysis. These tools enhance the accuracy and speed of medical diagnostics, supporting radiologists and clinicians.

Genomics and Drug Discovery: Clara includes solutions for genomics and drug discovery, leveraging GPU acceleration to analyze genomic data and simulate molecular interactions. The platform supports researchers in identifying genetic markers, understanding disease mechanisms, and discovering new drug candidates.

Integration with Healthcare Systems: Clara is designed to integrate with existing healthcare systems and workflows, enabling seamless adoption of AI technologies in clinical settings. The platform supports interoperability with medical imaging devices and electronic health records.

Nvidia Clara has made significant contributions to healthcare and life sciences by providing advanced AI tools and solutions. The platform has had the following impacts:

Enhanced Medical Diagnostics: Clara's AI-powered medical imaging tools have improved diagnostic accuracy and efficiency. Radiologists can use Clara's solutions to analyze medical images more quickly and identify abnormalities with greater precision.

Accelerated Drug Discovery: Clara's computational tools have accelerated the drug discovery process by enabling researchers to analyze large datasets and simulate molecular interactions. This acceleration has the potential to shorten the timeline for developing new treatments and therapies.

Personalized Medicine: Clara's genomics solutions support personalized medicine by enabling researchers to analyze genetic data and identify individual-specific disease risks and treatment options. This approach can lead to more tailored and effective healthcare interventions.

Nvidia Jarvis

Nvidia Jarvis is a conversational AI platform designed to enable the development and deployment of natural language processing (NLP) applications. The platform provides tools for building conversational agents, chatbots, and virtual assistants.

Nvidia Jarvis was introduced as part of Nvidia's AI platform portfolio and focuses on providing solutions for conversational AI. Key features of Jarvis include:

Speech Recognition: Jarvis includes advanced speech recognition capabilities that enable accurate transcription and understanding of spoken language. The platform supports various languages and accents, making it suitable for global applications.

Natural Language Understanding: Jarvis provides tools for natural language understanding (NLU), allowing developers to build conversational agents that can comprehend and respond to user queries effectively.

Text-to-Speech: Jarvis includes text-to-speech (TTS) capabilities that enable the generation of natural-sounding spoken responses. The TTS functionality supports various voices and languages, enhancing the user experience.

Customizable Models: Jarvis allows users to customize and fine-tune AI models for specific use cases and domains. Developers can train models on domain-specific data to improve accuracy and relevance.

Nvidia Jarvis has had a transformative impact on the field of conversational AI by providing advanced tools and capabilities. The platform has contributed to the following areas:

Enhanced User Interactions: Jarvis's speech recognition and natural language understanding capabilities have improved user interactions with conversational agents. Applications such as chatbots and virtual assistants can provide more accurate and context-aware responses.

Efficient Development: Jarvis's customizable models and pre-built components have streamlined the development of conversational AI applications. Developers can leverage Jarvis's tools to create and deploy AI-powered agents more quickly and effectively.

Industry Applications: Jarvis has been adopted in various industries, including customer service, healthcare, and finance, to enhance user engagement and support. The platform's conversational AI capabilities have enabled organizations to provide better customer support and automate routine tasks.

Nvidia's AI platforms, including DGX, Clara, and Jarvis, have played a crucial role in advancing AI technology and applications across industries. These platforms provide comprehensive solutions for AI development, deployment, and application, driving innovation and transformation in fields such as healthcare, automotive, and conversational AI. As AI continues to evolve, Nvidia's platforms will remain integral to shaping the future of technology and addressing emerging challenges and opportunities.

Transforming Industries with AI

Nvidia's AI technology has had a profound impact on various industries, driving innovation and transforming traditional practices. This section explores case studies of Nvidia's AI impact in key sectors, including healthcare, automotive, and robotics. These examples illustrate how Nvidia's AI solutions have addressed industry-specific challenges and enabled new possibilities.

Healthcare

The healthcare industry has undergone significant transformations due to advancements in AI, with Nvidia playing a central role in accelerating these changes. Nvidia's AI solutions have addressed challenges in medical imaging, genomics, and drug discovery, leading to improved diagnostics, personalized medicine, and accelerated research.

1. Medical Imaging

Nvidia's AI-powered medical imaging solutions have revolutionized the field of radiology and diagnostic imaging. The integration of AI technology has enhanced the accuracy and efficiency of image analysis, supporting radiologists in diagnosing and treating various conditions.

Case Study: IBM Watson Health

IBM Watson Health partnered with Nvidia to leverage AI for medical imaging and diagnostics. By using Nvidia's GPUs and AI algorithms, IBM Watson Health developed tools for analyzing medical images, such as MRI and CT scans. The AI-powered solutions improved image segmentation, detection of abnormalities, and diagnostic accuracy.

Key Benefits:

Enhanced Accuracy: AI algorithms can identify subtle abnormalities in medical images that may be missed by human eyes. This improved accuracy supports earlier detection and treatment of diseases.

Increased Efficiency: AI-powered tools automate image analysis, reducing the time required for radiologists to review and interpret images. This efficiency allows radiologists to focus on more complex cases and patient care.

Personalized Treatment: AI algorithms can analyze patient data and medical history to provide personalized treatment recommendations. This approach enables more targeted and effective therapies.

2. Genomics and Drug Discovery
Nvidia's Clara platform has played a significant role in accelerating genomics research and drug discovery. The platform's AI solutions support the analysis of genomic data, simulation of molecular interactions, and identification of potential drug candidates.

Case Study: NVIDIA Clara Genomics
Nvidia Clara Genomics is a comprehensive solution for genomics research, providing tools for analyzing genetic data and identifying genetic variations associated with diseases. The platform leverages Nvidia's GPUs to accelerate data processing and analysis.

Key Benefits:
Faster Analysis: Clara Genomics accelerates the processing of genomic data, reducing the time required for analyzing large-scale datasets. This acceleration supports rapid identification of genetic markers and disease associations.

Improved Accuracy: AI algorithms can identify genetic variations with high precision, leading to more accurate insights into disease mechanisms and potential therapeutic targets.

Accelerated Drug Discovery: Clara Genomics supports drug discovery by enabling simulations of molecular interactions and screening of potential drug candidates. This acceleration shortens the timeline for developing new treatments.

Automotive

The automotive industry has experienced significant changes due to the integration of AI technology, particularly in the development of autonomous vehicles and advanced driver-assistance systems (ADAS). Nvidia's AI solutions have played a crucial role in advancing these technologies and enhancing vehicle safety and performance.

1. Autonomous Vehicles

Nvidia's DRIVE platform provides a comprehensive solution for developing and deploying autonomous vehicle technologies. The platform includes hardware, software, and AI algorithms that enable vehicles to perceive their environment, make decisions, and navigate safely.

Case Study: Nvidia DRIVE and Tesla

Tesla has utilized Nvidia's DRIVE platform for developing its autonomous driving technology. The platform's GPUs and AI algorithms support Tesla's advanced driver-assistance features, such as Autopilot and Full Self-Driving (FSD).

Key Benefits:

Enhanced Perception: Nvidia's AI algorithms enable vehicles to process data from sensors, cameras, and lidar in real-time. This perception capability allows vehicles to detect and recognize objects, pedestrians, and road signs.

Improved Safety: AI-driven features, such as collision avoidance and adaptive cruise control, enhance vehicle safety by providing real-time alerts and automatic interventions. These features contribute to reducing accidents and improving overall road safety.

Autonomous Navigation: Nvidia's DRIVE platform supports autonomous navigation by enabling vehicles to make decisions based on environmental data. This capability allows for autonomous driving on highways and urban roads.

2. Advanced Driver-Assistance Systems (ADAS)
ADAS technologies have become increasingly prevalent in modern vehicles, providing features such as lane-keeping assistance, automatic emergency braking, and adaptive headlights. Nvidia's AI solutions have contributed to the development of these systems, enhancing vehicle safety and driver comfort.

Case Study: Nvidia and Volvo
Volvo has partnered with Nvidia to integrate AI technology into its ADAS offerings. The collaboration has led to the development of advanced safety features, such as automatic emergency braking and collision avoidance.

Key Benefits:
Enhanced Driver Assistance: AI-driven ADAS features provide real-time assistance to drivers, improving their ability to respond to potential hazards and maintain safe driving practices.

Increased Comfort: ADAS technologies contribute to a more comfortable driving experience by automating routine tasks and providing features such as adaptive cruise control and lane-keeping assistance.

Safety Improvement: The integration of AI into ADAS enhances vehicle safety by providing advanced warning systems and automatic interventions to prevent accidents.

Robotics
The field of robotics has also benefited from advancements in AI, with Nvidia's GPU technology supporting the development of intelligent and autonomous robots. AI-powered robots are used in

various applications, including manufacturing, logistics, and healthcare.

1. Robotics in Manufacturing

Nvidia's AI solutions have been applied to robotics in manufacturing, improving automation and efficiency in production processes. AI-powered robots can perform tasks such as assembly, quality control, and material handling with high precision and speed.

Case Study: Nvidia and Fanuc

Fanuc, a leading robotics company, has partnered with Nvidia to integrate AI into its industrial robots. The collaboration has led to the development of robots that can perform complex tasks with greater accuracy and adaptability.

Key Benefits:

Increased Precision: AI algorithms enable robots to perform manufacturing tasks with high precision, reducing defects and improving product quality.

Enhanced Efficiency: AI-powered robots can work at high speeds and handle complex tasks, increasing overall production efficiency and reducing downtime.

Adaptability: AI-driven robots can adapt to changing production requirements and perform a wide range of tasks, providing flexibility in manufacturing processes.

2. Robotics in Healthcare

AI-powered robots are also used in healthcare applications, including surgical assistance, rehabilitation, and patient care. Nvidia's AI solutions support the development of robots that can assist medical professionals and improve patient outcomes.

Case Study: Nvidia and Intuitive Surgical

Intuitive Surgical, a pioneer in robotic-assisted surgery, has collaborated with Nvidia to enhance its surgical robots with AI capabilities. The partnership has led to the development of advanced surgical systems that provide improved precision and control during procedures.

Key Benefits:

Enhanced Precision: AI-driven surgical robots provide precise control and accuracy during procedures, reducing the risk of complications and improving patient outcomes.

Improved Recovery: Robotic-assisted surgeries often result in shorter recovery times and reduced postoperative pain, benefiting patients and healthcare providers.

Increased Accessibility: AI-powered robots can assist in performing complex procedures, making advanced surgical techniques more accessible to patients and healthcare facilities.

Nvidia's AI technology has had a transformative impact on various industries, driving innovation and addressing industry-specific challenges. Through platforms like DGX, Clara, and Jarvis, and contributions to fields such as healthcare, automotive, and robotics, Nvidia has played a crucial role in shaping the future of AI and enabling new possibilities for technological advancement. As AI continues to evolve, Nvidia's solutions will remain integral to driving progress and addressing emerging opportunities across industries.

This comprehensive exploration of Nvidia's role in the AI revolution highlights the company's significant contributions to advancing AI technology and transforming various industries. Through innovations in GPU technology and the development of specialized AI platforms, Nvidia has played a pivotal role in shaping the future of AI and driving technological progress across multiple sectors.

Chapter 7:
The Future of Nvidia

Nvidia's Vision for the Future

Nvidia's trajectory has been significantly shaped by its co-founder and CEO, Jensen Huang. Since the company's inception, Huang has demonstrated visionary leadership that has propelled Nvidia from a niche graphics card manufacturer to a global leader in AI and computing technology. His strategic foresight and innovative approach have been pivotal in steering the company towards new horizons. This section delves into Huang's leadership style, Nvidia's strategic roadmap, and the company's vision for the future.

Jensen Huang's Leadership

Jensen Huang, a Taiwanese-American entrepreneur, has been at the helm of Nvidia since its founding in 1993. His leadership style is characterized by a combination of technical expertise, strategic thinking, and a strong commitment to innovation. Huang's ability to foresee technological trends and adapt the company's strategy accordingly has been instrumental in Nvidia's success.

Huang's visionary approach is evident in Nvidia's strategic decisions and technological advancements. His focus on the future of computing, AI, and graphics has guided Nvidia through multiple technology cycles, positioning the company as a leader in emerging fields. Huang's ability to anticipate market trends and technological shifts has enabled Nvidia to stay ahead of its competitors and seize new opportunities.

Under Huang's leadership, Nvidia has consistently prioritized innovation. The company's investments in research and development, coupled with Huang's emphasis on pushing the boundaries of technology, have led to groundbreaking advancements in GPU technology, AI, and data centers. Huang's commitment to innovation is reflected in Nvidia's product portfolio, which includes cutting-edge solutions for gaming, professional visualization, and AI.

Huang has been instrumental in forging strategic partnerships that have enhanced Nvidia's capabilities and market presence. Collaborations with companies such as Microsoft, Amazon, and Google have enabled Nvidia to leverage its technology in diverse applications, from cloud computing to autonomous vehicles. These partnerships have expanded Nvidia's reach and solidified its position as a key player in the tech industry.

A significant aspect of Huang's leadership is his focus on AI and computing. Recognizing the transformative potential of AI, Huang has steered Nvidia towards becoming a leading provider of AI infrastructure and solutions. The company's investments in AI research, development of AI platforms, and acquisition of AI-related companies underscore Huang's commitment to driving progress in this field.

Nvidia's Roadmap and Strategic Goals
Nvidia's roadmap for the future is shaped by its commitment to advancing technology and addressing emerging challenges. The company's strategic goals encompass several key areas, including AI, the Metaverse, and diversification into new markets.

1. Advancing AI Technology
Nvidia's roadmap places a strong emphasis on advancing AI technology. The company aims to further develop its AI platforms, such as DGX and Clara, to address evolving industry needs and support cutting-edge research. Nvidia's AI strategy includes enhancing its hardware and software solutions, expanding its AI ecosystem, and fostering collaboration with research institutions and industry leaders.

2. Developing the Metaverse

The concept of the Metaverse represents a significant opportunity for Nvidia to leverage its technology in creating immersive virtual worlds. Nvidia's roadmap includes investments in technologies that enable the development of the Metaverse, such as advanced graphics rendering, AI-driven virtual environments, and real-time simulation. The company's efforts in this area align with its vision of shaping the future of digital experiences and interactive media.

3. Expanding into New Markets

Nvidia's strategic goals also involve expanding into new markets and applications. The company is exploring opportunities in areas such as healthcare, automotive, and robotics, where its technology can drive innovation and address industry-specific challenges. Nvidia's diversification strategy includes developing solutions that cater to the unique needs of these markets and establishing a strong presence in emerging sectors.

4. Strengthening Ecosystem Partnerships

Strengthening ecosystem partnerships is another key aspect of Nvidia's roadmap. The company aims to enhance collaboration with technology providers, software developers, and industry stakeholders to create a robust ecosystem around its products and solutions. These partnerships are crucial for driving adoption, fostering innovation, and addressing complex challenges in technology and computing.

The Metaverse and Beyond

Nvidia's Role in Developing the Metaverse and Future Virtual Worlds

The Metaverse represents a new frontier in digital technology, encompassing a vast network of interconnected virtual environments where users can interact, socialize, and create. Nvidia's involvement in the development of the Metaverse and future virtual worlds highlights the company's commitment to shaping the next generation of digital experiences. This section explores Nvidia's role in the Metaverse, its contributions to virtual world development, and the potential impact of these technologies.

The Metaverse is a concept that envisions a collective virtual space where users can engage in various activities, such as gaming, socializing, and work. It combines elements of augmented reality (AR), virtual reality (VR), and digital twins to create immersive and interactive experiences. The Metaverse is expected to revolutionize how people interact with digital content and each other, offering new opportunities for entertainment, communication, and commerce.

Nvidia's Contributions to the Metaverse
Nvidia's technology plays a pivotal role in enabling the development of the Metaverse. The company's expertise in graphics processing, AI, and real-time simulation is essential for creating realistic and immersive virtual environments. Nvidia's contributions to the Metaverse include:

1. Advanced Graphics Rendering
Nvidia's GPUs are at the forefront of advanced graphics rendering, providing the computational power needed to create high-quality virtual environments. The company's graphics technology supports detailed textures, realistic lighting, and complex simulations, enhancing the visual fidelity of virtual worlds. Nvidia's RTX series GPUs, with features like real-time ray tracing, are particularly well-suited for creating lifelike virtual experiences.

2. AI-Driven Virtual Worlds

AI technology is integral to the development of interactive and dynamic virtual worlds. Nvidia's AI platforms, such as DGX and Clara, contribute to creating intelligent virtual environments that can adapt to user interactions and provide personalized experiences. AI-driven solutions enable realistic character behavior, responsive environments, and advanced content generation.

3. Real-Time Simulation

Real-time simulation is a key aspect of the Metaverse, allowing users to interact with virtual environments in real-time. Nvidia's technology supports real-time physics simulations, complex animations, and dynamic world interactions. This capability enhances the immersion and interactivity of virtual experiences, making them more engaging and realistic.

4. Collaboration with Industry Leaders

Nvidia collaborates with industry leaders and technology providers to advance Metaverse development. Partnerships with companies such as Epic Games and Unity Technologies leverage Nvidia's technology to create advanced virtual environments and interactive content. These collaborations help drive innovation and accelerate the development of Metaverse applications.

The Future of Virtual Worlds

The future of virtual worlds and the Metaverse presents exciting possibilities for technology and digital experiences. Nvidia's role in shaping this future involves exploring new technologies, addressing emerging challenges, and fostering innovation in virtual environments.

1. Enhanced Immersion and Interactivity

Future virtual worlds are expected to offer enhanced immersion and interactivity, driven by advancements in graphics, AI, and simulation technologies. Nvidia's ongoing research and development efforts focus on improving the realism and responsiveness of virtual environments, enabling more engaging and lifelike experiences.

2. Integration of AR and VR Technologies

The integration of augmented reality (AR) and virtual reality (VR) technologies is a key aspect of the Metaverse's evolution. Nvidia's technology supports the development of AR and VR applications, enabling seamless interaction between virtual and physical worlds. The company's advancements in AR and VR hardware and software contribute to creating more immersive and interactive experiences.

3. Expanding Applications and Use Cases

The Metaverse's potential extends beyond gaming and entertainment to include applications in areas such as education, healthcare, and remote work. Nvidia's technology supports the development of virtual environments for various use cases, including virtual classrooms, telemedicine, and collaborative workspaces. The expansion of applications highlights the versatility and impact of the Metaverse.

4. Addressing Challenges and Opportunities

The development of the Metaverse and virtual worlds also presents challenges and opportunities. Issues related to privacy, security, and digital equity must be addressed to ensure the responsible and inclusive growth of virtual environments. Nvidia's role in addressing these challenges involves collaborating with stakeholders, developing secure and ethical technologies, and promoting digital inclusivity.

Ongoing Challenges and Opportunities
Challenges Facing Nvidia

Despite its successes, Nvidia faces several challenges as it navigates the future of technology and computing. These challenges include industry competition, technological evolution, and regulatory considerations.

1. Industry Competition

The technology industry is highly competitive, with key players such as AMD, Intel, and other tech giants vying for market share. Nvidia faces competition in areas such as GPU technology, AI, and data centers. Maintaining a competitive edge requires continuous innovation, strategic partnerships, and a deep understanding of market trends.

2. Technological Evolution

Technological evolution presents both opportunities and challenges for Nvidia. Rapid advancements in AI, computing, and graphics technology require Nvidia to stay at the forefront of innovation. The company must address emerging trends and adapt its technology to meet evolving industry needs.

3. Regulatory Considerations

Regulatory considerations are increasingly important in the technology sector. Nvidia must navigate complex regulatory environments related to data privacy, antitrust issues, and technology standards. Ensuring compliance with regulations and addressing regulatory challenges are essential for the company's continued success.

Opportunities for Growth

Despite the challenges, Nvidia has significant opportunities for growth and advancement in various areas. These opportunities include expanding into new markets, driving innovation, and leveraging emerging technologies.

1. Expanding into New Markets

Nvidia's diversification strategy presents opportunities for growth in new markets, such as healthcare, automotive, and robotics. The company's technology can drive innovation and address industry-specific challenges, positioning Nvidia as a key player in emerging sectors.

2. Driving Innovation

Driving innovation is a core aspect of Nvidia's strategy. The company's focus on research and development, coupled with its commitment to technological advancement, creates opportunities for breakthrough innovations. Nvidia's continued investment in R&D and collaboration with industry leaders will drive progress and open new avenues for growth.

3. Leveraging Emerging Technologies

Emerging technologies, such as quantum computing and advanced AI, present opportunities for Nvidia to expand its technology portfolio and address new challenges. By leveraging these technologies, Nvidia can develop new solutions, explore novel applications, and maintain its leadership in the technology sector.

As Nvidia navigates the future of technology, its vision for innovation, expansion, and leadership will continue to shape its trajectory. Through visionary leadership, strategic goals, and a focus on emerging technologies, Nvidia is well-positioned to drive progress and address future challenges. The company's role in the Metaverse, AI revolution, and ongoing technological advancements highlights its commitment to shaping the future of computing and digital experiences. With a clear roadmap and a dedication to innovation, Nvidia's future promises to be dynamic and impactful, driving technological progress and creating new opportunities across industries.

Conclusion

Nvidia's journey from a modest startup to a global technology giant is a testament to its innovative spirit, strategic foresight, and relentless pursuit of excellence. Founded in 1993 by Jensen Huang, Chris Malachowsky, and Curtis Priem, Nvidia began as a small company focused on developing graphics processing units (GPUs) for gaming and professional visualization. The company's initial product lineup, including the RIVA series of graphics cards, laid the groundwork for its future success.

The pivotal moment in Nvidia's history came with the development of the GeForce 256, the world's first GPU, which revolutionized the graphics industry by integrating programmable shaders and real-time 3D rendering capabilities. This breakthrough positioned Nvidia as a leader in graphics technology and set the stage for its subsequent growth and diversification.

As Nvidia continued to innovate, it expanded its product offerings beyond traditional graphics cards. The company's strategic move into professional visualization, data centers, and automotive markets showcased its ability to leverage its core GPU technology for a broader range of applications. Nvidia's acquisition strategy, including the purchase of Mellanox Technologies and the attempted acquisition of ARM, further solidified its position as a dominant force in the tech industry.

Nvidia's foray into AI and deep learning marked a significant turning point. The introduction of CUDA (Compute Unified Device Architecture) and the development of specialized AI platforms, such as DGX, Clara, and Jarvis, demonstrated Nvidia's commitment to advancing AI technology and addressing complex computational challenges. The company's role in the AI revolution has transformed industries and driven significant progress in fields such as healthcare, automotive, and robotics.

Throughout its journey, Nvidia has faced challenges and controversies, including intense competition from rivals like AMD and Intel, legal battles, and regulatory scrutiny. Despite these obstacles, Nvidia's innovative solutions and strategic vision have enabled it to navigate the tech landscape successfully and maintain its leadership position.

Reflection on Nvidia's Impact on Technology and Society

Nvidia's impact on technology and society is profound and multifaceted. The company's contributions extend beyond the realm of graphics and computing, influencing various aspects of modern life and driving progress across multiple industries.

1. Revolutionizing Graphics and Gaming

Nvidia's advancements in GPU technology have fundamentally transformed the gaming industry. The company's graphics cards have enabled developers to create visually stunning and immersive gaming experiences, pushing the boundaries of what is possible in digital entertainment. Technologies such as real-time ray tracing and AI-driven graphics enhancements have set new standards for visual fidelity and realism in gaming.

2. Advancing AI and Machine Learning

Nvidia's innovations in AI and machine learning have had a transformative impact on various fields. The company's GPUs and AI platforms have accelerated research and development in areas such as natural language processing, computer vision, and autonomous systems. Nvidia's technology has empowered researchers, developers, and organizations to tackle complex problems and drive advancements in AI.

3. Enhancing Professional Visualization

In the realm of professional visualization, Nvidia's technology has enabled advancements in fields such as architecture, film production, and scientific research. The company's GPUs are used in high-performance computing environments to render detailed simulations, visualize complex datasets, and create realistic digital models. Nvidia's contributions have facilitated breakthroughs in design, animation, and scientific discovery.

4. Transforming Industries

Nvidia's impact extends to various industries, including healthcare, automotive, and robotics. In healthcare, Nvidia's AI platforms support medical imaging, drug discovery, and personalized medicine, improving patient outcomes and advancing medical research. In the automotive sector, Nvidia's technology is integral to the development of autonomous vehicles and advanced driver assistance systems. The company's contributions to robotics enhance automation and intelligent systems in various applications.

5. Shaping the Future of Digital Experiences

Nvidia's involvement in the development of the Metaverse and virtual worlds represents a new frontier in digital experiences. The company's technology enables the creation of immersive virtual environments, interactive simulations, and advanced digital interactions. Nvidia's role in shaping the future of the Metaverse reflects its commitment to driving innovation and expanding the possibilities of digital technology.

Speculation on What the Future Holds for Nvidia and Its Influence on the World

As Nvidia looks to the future, several trends and developments will likely shape the company's trajectory and influence on the world.

The following areas offer insights into what the future may hold for Nvidia and its impact on technology and society.

1. Continued Innovation in AI and Computing

Nvidia's commitment to innovation will likely drive further advancements in AI and computing. The company's ongoing research and development efforts will focus on enhancing its AI platforms, exploring new technologies, and addressing emerging challenges. Innovations in areas such as quantum computing, advanced AI algorithms, and next-generation GPUs will shape Nvidia's future and influence the broader tech landscape.

2. Expansion into New Markets

Nvidia's diversification strategy will continue to play a key role in the company's growth. Expanding into new markets, such as healthcare, automotive, and robotics, presents opportunities for Nvidia to leverage its technology and address industry-specific challenges. The company's ability to adapt its solutions to diverse applications will drive innovation and create new opportunities for growth.

3. Shaping the Metaverse and Virtual Worlds

The development of the Metaverse and virtual worlds represents a significant opportunity for Nvidia. The company's technology will play a crucial role in creating immersive virtual environments, enabling new forms of digital interaction, and driving the evolution of the Metaverse. Nvidia's contributions to virtual reality, augmented reality, and real-time simulation will influence the future of digital experiences and interactive media.

4. Addressing Ethical and Regulatory Challenges

As Nvidia continues to advance technology, addressing ethical and regulatory challenges will be essential. Issues related to data privacy, security, and digital equity will require careful consideration and proactive measures. Nvidia's approach to addressing these challenges will impact its reputation and influence the responsible development of technology.

5. Fostering Collaboration and Ecosystem Growth
Fostering collaboration with industry leaders, research institutions, and technology providers will be key to Nvidia's future success. Building a robust ecosystem around its products and solutions will drive innovation, promote adoption, and enhance Nvidia's impact across various sectors. The company's ability to collaborate effectively and engage with diverse stakeholders will shape its role in driving technological progress.

6. Driving Sustainability and Social Responsibility
Sustainability and social responsibility are increasingly important considerations for technology companies. Nvidia's efforts to address environmental and social challenges, such as reducing carbon emissions and promoting diversity and inclusion, will influence its future impact and reputation. The company's commitment to sustainability and responsible practices will shape its role as a technology leader and contribute to positive societal outcomes.

Nvidia's journey from a startup to a technology giant reflects its innovative spirit, strategic vision, and commitment to excellence. The company's impact on technology and society is profound, driving advancements in graphics, AI, professional visualization, and various industries. As Nvidia looks to the future, its continued focus on innovation, expansion, and addressing emerging challenges will shape its trajectory and influence on the world. With a clear vision, a dedication to advancing technology, and a commitment to responsible practices, Nvidia is poised to continue its role as a leading force in the tech industry and drive progress across multiple sectors.

www.ingramcontent.com/pod-product-compliance
Lightning Source LLC
LaVergne TN
LVHW051658050326
832903LV00032B/3884

* 9 7 9 8 3 4 1 3 0 7 2 5 4 *